# *The Quilter's Directory of Embellishments*

# The Quilter's Directory
# of Embellishments

## Sally Holman

C&T PUBLISHING

A QUARTO BOOK

First published in 2006 by
C&T Publishing Inc.
1651 Challenge Drive
Concord, CA 94520-5206
www.ctpub.com

ISBN-10: 1-57120-386-9
ISBN-13: 978-1-57120-386-1

Conceived, designed, and produced by
Quarto Publishing plc
The Old Brewery
6 Blundell Street
London N7 9BH

QUAR.WEQ

*Editor:* Karen Koll
*Art Editor:* Natasha Montgomery
*Assistant Art Director:* Penny Cobb
*Copy Editor:* Claire Wedderburn Maxwell
*Designers:* Karin Skånberg, Claire Van Rhyn,
Michelle Stamp
*Photographers:* Phillip Wilkins, Martin Norris
*Illustrator:* John Woodcock
*Indexer:* Diana LeCore

*Art Director:* Moira Clinch
*Publisher:* Paul Carslake

Manufactured by Modern Age Repro House Ltd., Hong Kong
Printed by SNP Leefung Holding Limited, China

# Contents

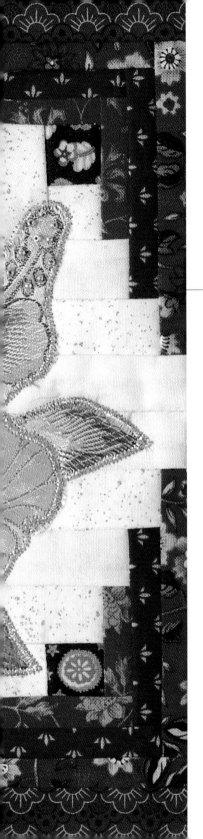

# Introduction

There are many practical and esthetic reasons for adding embellishments to quilted projects. Embellishments can highlight a specific area, add sparkle, detail, or decoration, or personalize a piece of work. They can cover raw edges, hide or decorate seams, help with color balance, and "tie" quilt layers together.

Embellishments can vary greatly in content and variety, from old to new, textiles to trinkets, and can include beads, buttons, sequins, charms, foils, lace, threads, and braids as well as found objects.

A variety of embellishments can be used to adorn and decorate quilts. Beads and sequins can be used to "tie" a quilt, add sparkle, or can be stitched into motifs to create a unique project. Embroidery is a wonderful way to add color and texture; it can be used to hide or define seams or as an alternative to classic quilting stitches. Lace, braids, ribbons, and cords can be made into flowers or couched along seams, while sheer fabrics such as organza or voile add shimmer. Metallic foil, fabric paints, and crayon can add interest to traditional block patterns, while computer printing will personalize projects.

This book will introduce you to the concept of embellishment, encourage you to explore its possibilities in quilt making, and help you to decide when, where, and how to add embellishments to your work.

## About this book

Each block featured in the Techniques section (pages 22–117) has been designed to illustrate a technique that can be used to embellish a quilt or quilt block. The introductory section (pages 10–21) discusses several quiltmaking techniques, and the Resources section (pages 124–125) suggests suppliers, books of block patterns, and other quiltmaking books.

## Gallery section

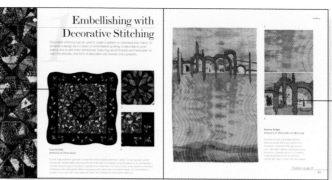

**Quilt gallery**
*Gallery pages are featured throughout the book whenever a new section begins. Be inspired by the work of leading quilters and see how single blocks can be put together to create whole quilts.*

**Details**
*Important embellishment details are pointed out.*

## Techniques section

**Featured block**
*For purposes of comparison, all featured blocks are made up as 9" (22cm) finished squares.*

**Other techniques**
*Although each new technique has its own block, some additional techniques are needed to complete certain blocks. Look at this section to find the complementary techniques.*

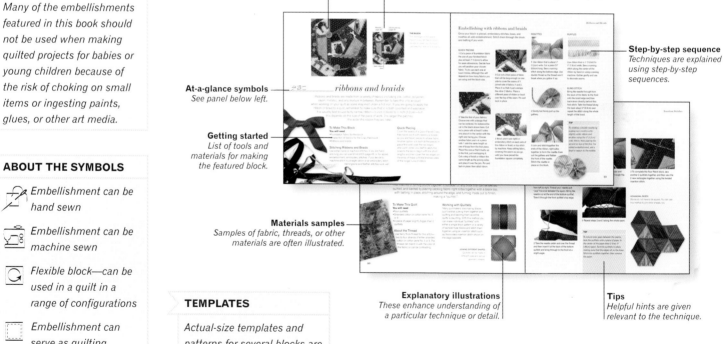

**At-a-glance symbols**
*See panel below left.*

**Getting started**
*List of tools and materials for making the featured block.*

**Step-by-step sequence**
*Techniques are explained using step-by-step sequences.*

**Materials samples**
*Samples of fabric, threads, or other materials are often illustrated.*

**Explanatory illustrations**
*These enhance understanding of a particular technique or detail.*

**Tips**
*Helpful hints are given relevant to the technique.*

### SAFETY

*Many of the embellishments featured in this book should not be used when making quilted projects for babies or young children because of the risk of choking on small items or ingesting paints, glues, or other art media.*

### ABOUT THE SYMBOLS

 *Embellishment can be hand sewn*

*Embellishment can be machine sewn*

*Flexible block—can be used in a quilt in a range of configurations*

*Embellishment can serve as quilting*

### TEMPLATES

*Actual-size templates and patterns for several blocks are found on pages 118–123.*

# Equipment

You do not need a lot of specialized equipment to try out many of the embellishment techniques featured in this book. However, a few good basic tools will make the processes easier and more successful, while a few specialized tools are required for some of the more complicated techniques.

**NEEDLES**

You will need a selection (see chart) of different sizes and different types of good-quality needles (poor-quality or blunt needles may damage the fabric or thread).

**PINS**

There are many different types of pins available, from basic dressmaker's pins to long quilter's pins and fancy flat-headed (or flower-headed) pins. The best pins to use are long, narrow, sharp, good-quality pins that do not damage the fabric's surface.

**THIMBLES**

You may find it helpful to wear a thimble. There are many different types available, so try a few and choose one that fits you well and is comfortable.

## Needle types and sizes

The size and type of needle you need will depend on the fabric, thread, and type of stitching you are doing. Make sure you match the thickness of the thread to the size of the needle's eye—this will aid threading and avoid damaging the thread.

| TYPE | PURPOSE | SIZE |
| --- | --- | --- |
| Sharps | General sewing | Available in various lengths and sizes |
| Betweens | Quilting (can be useful for some beading) | Short length, various sizes |
| Embroidery | Embroidery/general sewing | Various lengths, long eye, sharp point, mixed sizes |
| Crewel | Fine and medium-weight embroidery | Medium length, sharp point |
| Chenille | Silk or other ribbon | Similar to crewel but with larger eyes to accommodate heavier threads or ribbon |
| Tapestry | Weaving or very coarse thread on canvas | Blunt point that does not snag on fabrics if using for weaving |
| Beading | Stitching on tiny seed beads | Fine, long needles, various sizes |

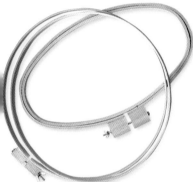

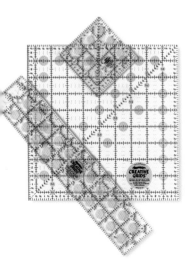

### MARKERS

Nonpermanent markers such as quilter's pencils (available in silver and white), No. 2 pencils, and dressmaker's carbon can all be used to transfer stitching lines or motif patterns onto fabric. Always try out your chosen marker first on the fabric you are using to make sure that it is erasable before you mark your whole piece.

Iron-on transfer pencils transfer a permanent mark onto fabric. The image is drawn onto cooking parchment paper and pressed with a hot iron with the marked side on the right side of the fabric. The mirror image of the original pattern transfers to the fabric.

### SCISSORS

Ideally you need three pairs of scissors: small embroidery scissors, larger scissors for cutting fabric, and scissors for cutting paper. Buy good-quality scissors with a sharp, accurate cut.

### FRAMES AND HOOPS

Frames and hoops are important tools for keeping work flat while you are stitching and/or hand quilting. Both hand-held and free-standing frames are available. Embroidery hoops are made from narrower wood than quilting frames, while plastic, snap-together frames can be used for both quilting and embroidery.

### RULER

You can purchase a number of different sizes of quilt rulers that can be used for pattern drafting, measuring, and marking fabric. The wider rulers can also be used with a rotary cutter and cutting board.

## Sewing machines

Some sewing machines are capable of creating not only rows of embroidery but also motifs in different sizes, colors, and designs, but even fairly basic models can be used for a number of embellishment techniques.

### WHAT TO LOOK FOR IN A SEWING MACHINE

- Useful stitches: a variety of embroidery stitches.
- Useful feet: free-motion foot, open-ended embroidery foot, cording foot, and walking foot.
- Useful features: needle in/needle out, good-sized machine table.
- Useful equipment: good selection of quality needles for different types of threads and fabrics, selection of bobbins wound with different colored threads.

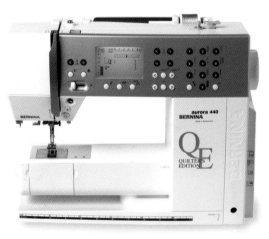

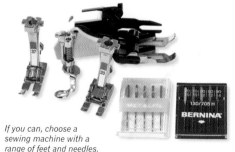

*If you can, choose a sewing machine with a range of feet and needles.*

# _Choosing fabrics and embellishments_

Embellished quilts can be made from nearly endless combinations of fabrics and embellishments. Mix fabrics for exciting and challenging results, and top off the project with embellishment richness or glitz.

## Fabrics

### COTTON

Craft weight cotton is produced specifically for making quilts. It is simple and reliable to use, and can be bought in many patterns, colors, and finishes. Other cotton fabrics are muslin, calico, and cotton sateen.

### COTTON LAMÉ

Cotton with lamé (a synthetic) woven through it gives the fabric many of the properties of cotton but with a shimmer. Be careful to use a cool iron with cotton lamé as it can scorch.

### SILK

Silk comes in many different types and colors, from dupion silk, which is rich and shiny, to silk noile, which is textured and matte in finish. Combinations of silks can create wonderful textured effects. Note, however, that silk frays easily, so take care and add extra seam allowances.

### SYNTHETIC FABRICS

The category of synthetic fabrics includes everything from polyester cotton to some of the shiny jersey fabrics. These fabrics can be difficult to use, as they tend to be slippery or stretchy and may need stabilizing with a foundation fabric or require a backing of lightweight iron-on interfacing. Take care when pressing.

### SHEER FABRICS

Made from cotton, synthetic fibers, or both, sheer fabrics can shade colors, diffuse color, "trap" embellishments between layers, cover raw edges as in shadow quilting, or make embellishments. Sheer fabrics may scorch, so press them carefully.

### RECYCLED FABRICS

Some wonderful vintage fabrics can be found in thrift stores and given a new life in a quilt.

# Embellishments

### CHARMS

Found in metal, glass, plastic, resin, and ceramic, charms personalize a quilt, often adding novelty or linking the project to a theme. Usually stitched in place or tied with ribbon and then stitched, they are easy to apply. They can be purely decorative or used as quilting, but should not be used on quilts for babies or young children.

### LACE

Lace is a particularly attractive embellishment. Cream or white lace can lighten the color of fabric for a softer look, and old lace lends a vintage feeling to modern fabrics. Use lace to cover seams, diffuse color, or add themed details (using lace motifs of flowers, butterflies, and so on). Lace also makes very pretty appliqué.

### BEADS

Available in all shapes and sizes and in materials as diverse as plain glass, fancy glass, crystal, plastic, ceramic, and wood, beads can both decorate a quilt and tie it together. The simple techniques do require good eyesight and nimble fingers, but pay off in sparkle and interest, richness and luxury, livening up dull fabric and highlighting stitch patterns. Beads should not be used on quilts for babies or young children.

### RIBBONS

Ribbons can tie a quilt together, cover seams, serve as fabric, or embellish as bows, weaving, ribbon flowers, or embroidery. Available in many materials and widths, it is sometimes possible to find vintage ribbons. Ribbons require careful laundering and should not be used on quilts for babies or young children.

### BUTTONS

Varied and versatile, buttons can give a country feel in folk-art quilts, a vintage look from mother-of-pearl buttons, and a modern look from novelty themed buttons. Simple and effective decoration, they also serve a functional purpose if used to tie the quilt together. Stitch on with beads or thread ties for further embellishment. Certain types of buttons shouldn't be laundered (i.e. metal or wood), and buttons are not always colorfast. Don't use on quilts for babies or young children.

### SEQUINS

Sequins can decorate embroidery stitches, cover raw edges, and glint from underneath sheer fabric. Themed shaped sequins (flowers, leaves, butterflies) and sequins stitched into flower shapes add to the story of a pictoral or personalized quilt block. Sequins are not always colorfast and can be time consuming to attach, but they add sparkle and richness ranging from elegant to fun in mood. Don't use on quilts for babies or young children.

### FOUND OBJECTS

The found objects category encompasses anything not specifically made for embellishment. Items from the natural world are nice additions (shells, feathers, twigs), and recycled items can be versatile (netting from packaged fruit). Many found objects must be attached with glue, so they are suitable only for items that will not be laundered. Found objects should not be used on quilts for babies or young children.

### FOILS

These foils, specially designed for application to fabric, give a "gilded" appearance to the surface of a quilt. They are available in gold, copper, silver, and other colors, including some with fancy finishes. Using foils, which are applied with a flexible glue or fusible web, requires prac   ,  a  d they are best used on seldom-laundered pieces. They give an artistic effect to a quilt, and can look antiquarian. Glues used with foils could be hazardous to babies or young children.

### FABRIC PAINTS

Fabric paints can color a whole piece of fabric or can be used to stamp or paint a motif. They come in many colors and finishes, the basic types including opaque, metallic, and pearlescent. A basic set of paints allows you to create interesting fabric from basics like cotton, saving on fabric costs. Painting can be messy and requires a lot of preparation, but it offers great creative options. Don't use on quilts for babies or young children.

### FABRIC CRAYONS

With fabric crayons, you can transfer a drawing or tracing onto fabric to make anything from a large block centerpiece to a tiny repeated motif. Crayons are cleaner and quicker to use than paints, although it can be difficult to get a clear, deep image. This is a great choice for an artistic, personal effect. Don't use on quilts for babies or young children.

13

# *Utility fabrics and threads*

Utility fabrics such as interfacing, stabilizer fabrics, fusible web, and batting are not very often on show once a quilt project has been completed but are nevertheless an important part of its construction. Threads are also an important part of your quilt whether used for piecing or for decorative features.

## Interfacing

Interfacing is a dressmaking fabric used to add stiffness to collars, cuffs, and shirt fronts. There are two main types of interfacing: sew-in interfacing and iron-on interfacing. These can be purchased as lightweight, medium-weight, and heavy or craft-weight interfacing. They are best used as follows:

- Lightweight sew-in interfacing is best as a foundation fabric for foundation piecing.
- Medium-weight sew-in interfacing is ideal as a stabilizer for machine embroidery.
- Lightweight iron-on interfacing is best as a stabilizer for stretchy or fine fabrics or as a backing for quick-turn appliqué.

**Tip:** When using iron-on interfacing, always test it on a small piece of your chosen fabric first to make sure that when pressed it does not mark the front of the fabric.

## Stabilizer fabrics

Machine embroidery often puckers if stitched through only one layer of fabric, so you need to place a stabilizer fabric underneath. If the work has been foundation pieced onto interfacing this will act as the stabilizer, and if you are "quilting as you go" through batting this will also prevent puckering. If, however, you are stitching a motif onto a single layer of fabric, you should use tear-off stabilizer underneath the fabric.

*Above from top: interfacing and stabilizer fabric*

## Fusible web

Fusible web is used to bond two fabrics together and can be purchased in different widths, types, and strengths including heavy or light hold. You can purchase fusible web that is suitable for sewing through afterward or the no-sew variety.

Always read the instructions for the particular brand that you are using.

*Fusible web*

## Batting

Batting goes between the top of the quilt and the backing and provides warmth and texture when quilted. It is available in different weights, types, and widths.

Lightweight, low-loft batting in either cotton, polycotton, or polyester is ideal for embellished projects as it is easy to handle and stitch through and does not add too much weight to your projects.

Batting is produced by many different manufacturers and each type of batting has different properties. Read the care instructions when you buy your batting.

### COTTON BATTING

Cotton batting is easy to quilt but usually needs prewashing to allow for shrinkage. If you want a vintage look, do not prewash but let the batting shrink with the first washing of the quilt.

### POLYCOTTON BATTING

Polycotton batting is usually made up of 20 percent polyester and 80 percent cotton. It needs

*An array of batting samples*

prewashing and can be a little firmer to quilt than pure cotton.

## LOW-LOFT POLYESTER BATTING

Low-loft polyester batting is both light and easy to use. Needle-punched batting is best for most embellished quilts. Note that cheap polyester batting can "beard," when bits of batting rise to the top of the quilt, so always buy good-quality batting.

## POLYESTER BATTING

Polyester batting (4 oz/100g) is useful for comforter quilts that are usually tied and not quilted. Make sure that you buy a good-quality bonded or needle-punched batting that can be quilted a good distance apart.

## WOOL BATTING

This relatively new batting is warm and very soft and light.

## Threads

There are many different brands of machine sewing and hand sewing threads. They all have different effects when stitched, so consider the fabric you're using and the decorative effect that you require when choosing thread.

Remember also to match your needle to the thread—use a fine needle for fine thread and fine fabric. Special machine needles are available for use with metallic thread and these have larger, rounder eyes to stop the thread from shredding.

To achieve good-quality machine embroidery it is essential to use good-quality thread that flows with ease through your machine and gives good stitch cover.

You can use the same bobbin thread and top thread in your machine unless your top thread is specialized (such as metallic). If that is the case, your bobbin thread should be a good-quality cotton or polyester thread that is a similar or matching color.

*Threads for hand sewing*

## Threads for hand sewing

### STRANDED COTTON

This lustrous six-stranded yarn is widely available in many colors. You can also purchase hand-dyed (plain or space-dyed) stranded cotton from specialist outlets.

### STRANDED METALLIC

This shiny six-stranded thread is found in a limited range of plain colors, but new variegated and other special finished threads are now also available.

### STRANDED SILK

This soft and lustrous six-stranded yarn is available in a wide range of plain colors.

### COTTON PERLE

This single-stranded thread is available in a range of different thicknesses from No. 3 to No. 12 (12 is the finest). It is widely available in plain and variegated colors and you can also purchase hand-dyed cotton perle from specialist suppliers.

### SILK PERLE

Single-stranded silk perle is a soft, twisted yarn with a soft sheen. It is available from specialist suppliers in a variety of thicknesses and colors.

### RAYON

This very shiny six-stranded thread is available in a range of colors and is a good substitute for metallic colors. You can also buy hand-dyed rayon from specialist suppliers.

## Threads for machine sewing

### COTTON

Cotton thread comes in different weights and is sometimes space dyed. It is easy to use and gives a matte finish.

### POLYESTER OR POLYESTER SPUN WITH COTTON

Polyester or polycotton thread is easy to use and shinier than cotton.

### RAYON

Rayon thread is finer than cotton or polyester and very shiny. It covers well.

### SILK

Silk thread is fine with a good sheen.

### METALLIC

Metallic thread has a shiny finish and can be difficult to handle.

### HOLOGRAPHIC

Holographic thread has a special finish and produces an interesting effect.

*Threads for machine sewing*

# *Foundation piecing*

Foundation piecing is a method of piecing blocks together by sewing pieces onto a backing fabric or a tear-away paper. Lightweight sew-in interfacing (page 14) is ideal for this technique as it stabilizes the fabric for any embroidery.

1 Trace the pattern onto the foundation fabric or paper using a soft pencil. You may wish to mark the numbers onto the fabric (very lightly if you are

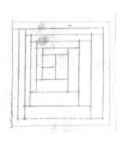

using light-colored fabric) to indicate the correct sewing sequence, or use your original pattern as the sequence guide. Remember to add at least ¼" (0.6cm) seam allowance all the way around the outside edge of the pattern. Pin the pattern down when tracing to stop it from slipping.

2 Cut out the individual fabric pieces for each marked section, adding at least ¼" (0.6cm) seam allowance to the finished (printed)

size. Unlike in classic piecing, these pieces do not have to be precisely measured as the foundation pattern is the accurate piece.

**TIP**

*Allow generous seam allowances, otherwise when you flip the fabric over you may not have enough fabric for the patch you are covering.*

3 Starting with piece 1, place it on the unmarked side of the foundation fabric with the right side of the fabric facing upward. It should cover

pattern area 1 plus a seam allowance.

Place a pin along the line where area 1 meets area 2. Remember that the fabric is placed on the **unmarked** side of the foundation base fabric and the pieces are stitched on the **marked** side. The picture, when finished, is therefore a reverse of the pattern.

Using the pin as a guide, with right sides together place pattern piece 2 with pattern piece 1 (i.e. along where 1 meets 2), overlapping the seam allowances. Pin through all the layers. Check that the pattern pieces cover areas 1 and 2 by flipping the fabric over to check. Sew along the drawn line by hand or machine.

4 Turn the foundation fabric or paper back over, and press.

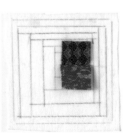

5 Repeat as for pattern piece 2 with the remaining numbered pieces until you have finished the pattern.

Remember to trim the seams if necessary as you go.

6 Press the piece of patchwork and then trim the outer edges, leaving at least a ¼" (0.6cm) seam allowance around the edge. If you have used foundation paper, tear it away.

# Classic block piecing

In classic block piecing, you cut paper templates as directed by a block pattern, and then use the templates to cut the fabric pieces that make up the block. Your block pattern book will guide you in assembling the pieces.

1 Using the templates necessary for your block, cut out the fabric pieces accurately, marking a ¼" (0.6cm) seam allowance. Remember to cut pieces on the straight grain of the fabric as indicated on the templates.

2 Start by stitching the pieces to make small units. For example, stitch together the 2 triangles to make a square. Matching the seams, pin the corners and the center. Stitch along the marked seam line. Press the seams either in one direction or open depending on the pattern and placement.

**TIP**

*Many quilters choose to cut their fabric pieces with a rotary cutter and ruler rather than with templates. To cut a quantity of squares and triangles, for example, you would cut a strip of fabric of the correct width (including seam allowances), cut across it to make squares, and cut across the squares to make triangles. So if your pieced squares are to be 2" (5cm), the squares to cut into half-square triangles should be 2⅞" (8.5cm). Many quilt pattern books give directions in this way.*

3 Place the pieces of the block in sequence. Sew together in a logical sequence (for example in rows), avoiding any insertion seams (see Tip at right). Press.

**TIP**

*If you are making a block pattern like the Le Moyne Star (page 38) you will need to sew an insertion seam. This is not difficult but it does need to be done correctly. At step 2, when stitching the pieces together, sew only to the start of the marked seam allowance (not into it). This will allow you to pivot the pieces when inserting the squares and triangles.*

# *Applied patchwork*

In applied patchwork, a pieced, patchwork motif is stitched to a backing
fabric. The motif can be machine pieced, or hand pieced over papers as
in English piecing. It can be hand sewn to the backing with blind stitch
or a decorative choice such as blanket stitch, or machine stitched.

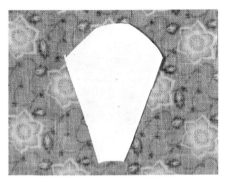

1 Cut out the block templates from freezer
paper.

3 Tack the fabric to the paper and whipstitch
the pieces together. Or stitch the pieces
together by machine straight stitch (above),
only to the end of the template at the curved
end, or by hand using running stitch. Press.

5 Using blind stitch (page 49), attach the
patchwork to the base square. Attach any
further patches in the same way.

2 Press the templates onto the back of the
fabric. Cut out adding a ¼" (0.6cm) seam
allowance.

4 If you have used the alternative stitching
method in step 3, tack the fabric over the
curved edges of the pieces.

# *Fusible appliqué*

Fusible appliqué involves bonding an appliqué motif to backing fabric using fusible web. The raw edges are then covered with machine or hand stitches or couching. This method reverses the drawn image.

1 Draw the appliqué motif onto the paper side of the fusible web. Roughly cut out the shape, leaving at least ¼" (0.6cm) outside the drawn lines.

3 Cut out the appliqué motif along the drawn line.

5 Hand or machine stitch around the edges of the motif. Satin stitch and blanket stitch work well. See page 52 for instructions on covering appliqué with couching.

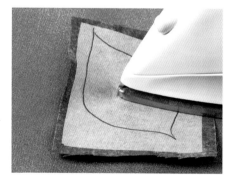

2 With the adhesive (non-paper) side of the fusible web facing downward onto the back of the fabric, press the paper side with an iron. This will transfer the adhesive web to the back of your fabric. Check the fusible web instructions for pressing temperatures and whether you need to use a damp cloth when pressing. Allow to cool.

4 Remove the backing paper and press the appliqué motif, sticky side down, in the correct position onto the right side of the fabric that it is being applied to.

# Quilting

Quilting is the process of stitching together the three layers that make up what is known as a "quilt sandwich": the top, batting, and backing. There are different ways of quilting by hand or machine. The blocks in this book have been quilted using several different quilting techniques, some of which are discussed here.

**OUTLINE QUILTING (HAND OR MACHINE)**

The stitches follow the shape of the fabric piece or motif, usually about ¼" (0.6cm) away from the edge. Embroidery outline quilting, as here, is often on the seam.

**ECHO QUILTING (HAND OR MACHINE)**

Several rows of the quilting stitches follow (echo) the outline of a shape, either the same distance apart or graduated to give a ripple effect.

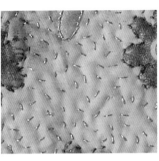

**SEED QUILTING (HAND)**

Small individual stitches that are all the same length are made at different angles over the area to be quilted.

**MACHINE QUILTING**

Machine quilting can be applied to many of the types of quilting, but instead of stitching by hand you use your sewing machine. You can quilt straight or curved lines, experiment with embroidery stitches, or use the special quilting stitch now featured on some sewing machines.

Free-motion quilting uses a special foot and can be used for stitching around motifs, echo quilting, and meander quilting.

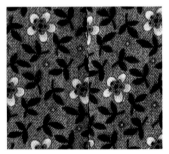

**IN-THE-DITCH QUILTING (HAND OR MACHINE)**

The quilting stitches sit directly over the seams and are therefore almost invisible.

**QUILTING WITH MOTIFS OR STENCILS (HAND)**

Running stitch or another embroidery stitch follows a quilting pattern previously drawn onto the fabric or block.

**TIED QUILTING (HAND)**

The layers are stitched together using knots, which can be combined with a button, bead, or other embellishment.

*The quilt sandwich*

# How to quilt successfully

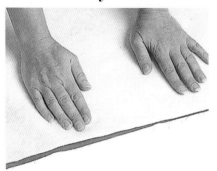

- Cut the batting and backing slightly larger than the block or quilt that you are quilting.

- Hand quilt using a frame or hoop to avoid puckering.

- Pin and then tack the 3 layers together vertically through the center, horizontally through the center, and then diagonally each way. If it is a large quilt you will need to tack from top to bottom and side to side in a grid-like formation a few inches (or centimeters) apart. A quilt frame with rollers lets you avoid the tacking process, as once the layered work is on the rollers it can be adjusted for tension.
- Always use good-quality threads and needles. Small, fine needles will encourage small, even stitches.
- Always try out your thread on scrap fabric first to see the effect it will create before you stitch your work. This saves unpicking and the subsequent unwanted holes and marks on your work.

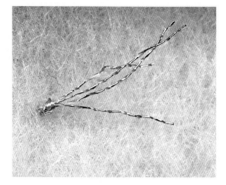

- If you are working through all the layers, "pop" the knot through the backing so that it is hidden in the batting.
- If you find it difficult to keep small stitches even, use thicker thread and larger stitches. Large and even stitches will look better than small but uneven ones.

*Good-quality threads and needles will lead to a better finished product.*

# Techniques

A variety of embellishment techniques have been used to make the blocks featured in this book, and these are explained in this section. You can use these to help you make your own blocks. The blocks used to illustrate the various types of embellishment have either been embellished during the piecing process, afterward, or both during and afterward.

# Embellishing with Decorative Stitching

Decorative stitching can be used to create a pattern on otherwise plain fabric, to enhance a design as in classic or embroidered quilting, to decorate or cover seams, and to add color and texture. Featuring varied threads and hand-sewn or machine stitches, this form of decoration can enliven many projects.

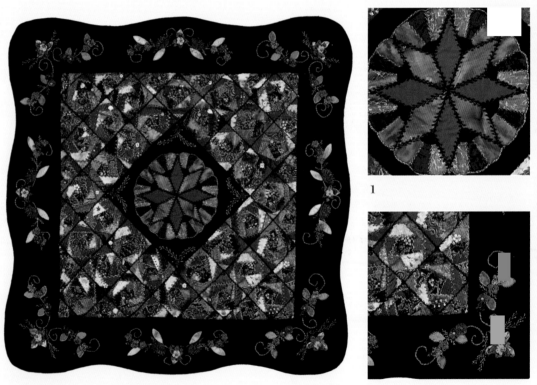

1

2

**Crazy for Color**
*dimensions 30" (76cm) square*

A small crazy medallion quilt with a pieced fan and star applied patchwork center. The star has been outline stitched with beaded feather stitch and the fans have been embroidered along the seams (1). A cord has been couched along the edge of the fans to highlight the curved lines. The corners of the center medallion have been embellished with embroidered ribbon roses along with beaded and embroidered leaves. This floral theme is echoed in the border with raised appliqué flowers with beaded and embroidered details (2).

1

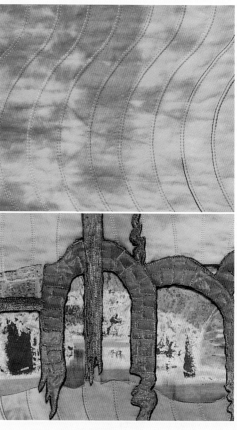

2

**Summer Bridges**
*dimensions 22" (56cm) wide x 34" (86cm) long*

A wholecloth quilt, hand dyed and then
machine quilted with a twin needle (1) to
emphasize movement of the lazy summer
river. Hand-dyed organza is appliquéd across
the bottom. Solarized photos of a Cotswold
bridge are printed on silk (2), and then
overlaid with layers of Kunin felt and organza.

*Continues on page 26*

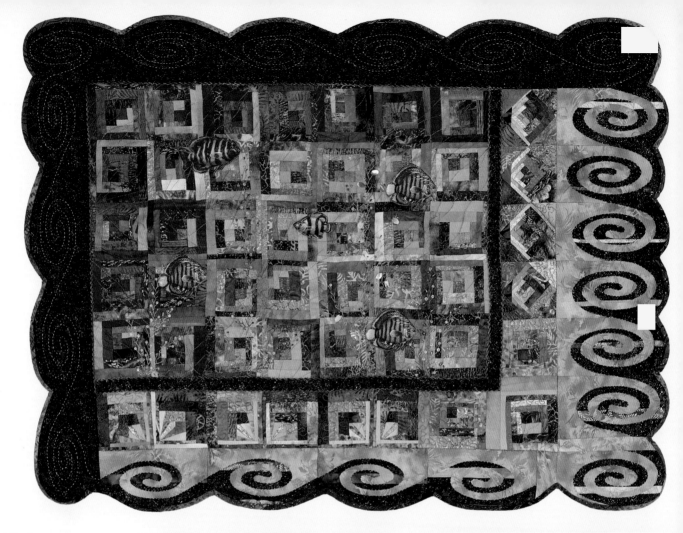

## Coral Reef

*dimensions 45" (114cm) wide x 34" (86cm) long*

A thick and thin foundation-pieced Log Cabin quilt (1) inspired by the colors of the coral reef. Hand and machine stitched, it features bonded appliqué fish cut from commercial fabrics and hand embroidered free-form feather stitch embellished with bead and sequin seaweed (2). The borders add bright green ocean plants (3) and swirling waves, appliquéd and then echoed in the quilting (4).

**1**

**3**

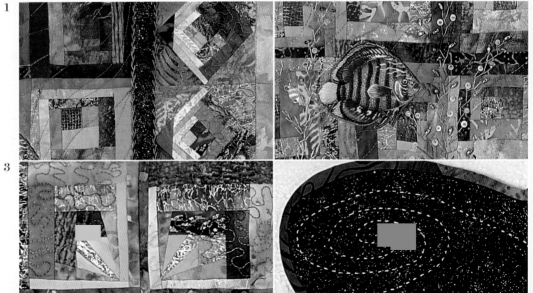

## Photo Opportunity
*dimensions 36" (91cm) wide x 44" (111cm) long*

A textured landscape that incorporates photographed images that have been transferred onto special fabric. They are used as whole pictures in the images around the edge (1) and as cut-out appliqué for the main picture (2). The small pictures have been quilted and stitched using colonial knots, running stitch, and feather stitch to highlight areas of the pictures. The printed images of gorse bushes on the main picture along with other details have been embroidered to bring out the colors and highlight the detail (3). The Storm at Sea border has been outline quilted using feather stitch (4).

Spider's web motif, page 32

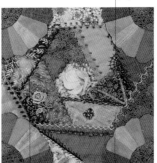

**CRAZY BLOCK**

This is a classic Crazy block, made up of random pieces, with fan corners. Each seam is embroidered using a variety of stitches and threads. If you embroider through the batting this will add additional texture and interest.

Double feather stitch, page 30

Chevron stitch with knots, page 29

# *hand embroidery stitches*

Embroidery stitches are used in Crazy patchwork to cover and decorate seams and to add motifs to the patches. They can be used in other types of patchwork as a decorative way of covering raw edges, outlining patches, to add texture or special features, or as an alternative to basic quilting.

## To Make This Block
### You will need
- Pieced block
- Embroidery threads
- Embroidery needles (page 10)
- Embroidery or quilting frame to hold your work flat

## About the Threads

Stranded cotton or stranded silk, cotton perle or silk perle, metallic threads or rayon threads are all suitable for embroidery. They can be plain or variegated, space dyed or hand dyed, shiny or dull, thick or fine. You can blend two or more threads together, for instance a fine metallic thread and stranded cotton. In fact, you can use any kind of thread that can be passed through a needle and fabric. Use two or three strands.

## Block Assembly

For best results, embroider through both the Crazy patchwork and a layer of batting. Use a fine, low-loft batting that will add weight and stability to your work without adding bulk. Add the backing fabric once the work has been embroidered but before you stitch on any embellishments as these will "tie" the front of the patchwork to the back. You can therefore use a knot at the end of your thread to start with as this will be hidden in between the batting and the backing. If you do embroider through all three quilt layers— the top, batting, and backing—make sure that you "pop" the knot through the backing fabric so that it is hidden in between the layers.

# Embellishing with embroidery stitches

Ideas for using embroidery stitches in blocks appear throughout this section. Following are a few of the most popular embroidery stitches that you can use.

## HERRINGBONE STITCH
This stitch should fall evenly on each side of the seam and is stitched from side to side.

1 Bring the needle through from the back to the front of the fabric below the guideline at 1. Make a small horizontal stitch above the guideline from right (at 2) to left (at 3).

3 Repeat this stitch sequence (6, 7, 8, and 9), keeping the stitches even.

## CHEVRON STITCH
This stitch should fall evenly on each side of the seam and is stitched from side to side.

2 Cross down to below the guideline. Insert the needle at 4 and make a small stitch of equal length to the stitch between 2 and 3, taking the needle out at 5 (this should be directly below 2).

1 Bring the needle through from the back to the front of the fabric below the guideline at 1. Make a small horizontal stitch above the guideline from right (at 2) to left (at 3). Make a small stitch from 4 to 5, bringing the needle out at 5 on top of point 2.

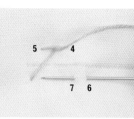

2 You should have a bar (from 3 to 4) on top of the stitch. The thread should be below the bar. Cross the thread down and insert the needle at 6. Make a small stitch of equal length to 4-5 above, coming out at 7.

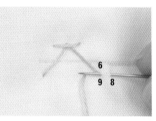

3 Complete the bar stitch by taking the needle through at 8 and back out at 9, on top of point 6.

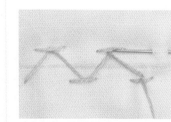

4 Repeat the above stitch sequence, stitching evenly.

## OPEN CRETAN STITCH
This stitch should fall evenly on each side of the seam and is stitched from side to side.

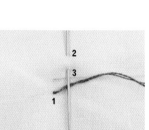

1 Bring the needle through from the back to the front of the fabric at 1. Take the needle through to the back at 2 then bring to the front at 3, making sure that the thread is under the needle as you pull it through. This stitch is above the line.

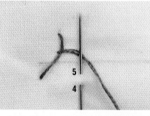

2 Take the needle through to the back at 4 then bring to the front at 5, making sure that the thread is under the needle as you pull it through. This stitch is below the line. Repeat the stitch sequence, keeping the stitches even.

*Continues on page 30*

## BASIC FEATHER STITCH

This stitch should fall evenly on each side of the seam and is stitched from top to bottom.

1 Bring the needle through from the back to the front of the fabric at 1. Take the needle back through at 2 and bring to the front again at 3. The thread should be under the needle as you pull it through at 3. Point 2 should be directly opposite point 1. Point 3 should be lower down, halfway between 1 and 2.

2 Take the needle through to the back at 4 then bring to the front at 5. The thread should be under the needle as you pull it through at 5. Point 4 should be directly opposite point 3. Point 5 should be lower down, halfway between 3 and 4.

3 Repeat to form an even, continuous line of stitches.

## DOUBLE FEATHER STITCH

This stitch is made in a similar way to basic feather stitch except that 2 stitches are made on each side at a slight angle. Triple feather stitch is also made in a similar way, but has 3 stitches on each side.

1 Bring the needle through from the back to the front of the fabric at 1. Take the needle back through at 2 and bring to the front again at 3. The thread should be under the needle as you pull it through at 3.

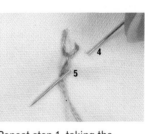

2 Repeat step 1, taking the needle back through at 4 and bringing it to the front at 5. The thread should be under the needle as you pull it through at 5.

3 Take the needle back through at 6 and bring to the front at 7. The thread should be under the needle as you pull it through.

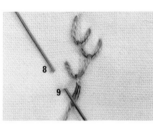

4 Take the needle back through at 8 and bring to the front at 9. The thread should be under the needle as you pull it through. Repeat these steps to stitch a continuous, even row.

## FEATHERED CHAIN STITCH

This stitch should fall evenly on each side of the seam and is stitched from top to bottom.

1 Bring the needle through from the back to the front of the fabric at 1. Take the needle back through next to 1 and bring to the front at 2, making sure that the thread passes under the needle. This is a chain stitch.

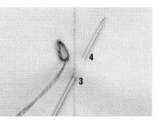

2 Take the needle back through at 3 (on the center line) and bring to the front at 4.

3 Take the needle back through next to 4 and bring to the front at 3, making sure that the thread passes under the needle as you pull it through. You have formed another chain stitch.

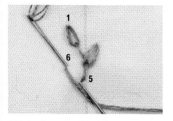

4 Take the needle back through at 5 (below 2) and come up at 6 (below 1). This will make the straight stitch. Then take the needle back through at 6 and bring up at 5, making sure that the thread passes under the needle as you pull it through. Repeat these steps to stitch a continuous, even row.

## LAZY DAISY
Lazy daisy can be stitched in pairs to create a row of leaves, in circles to make flowers, in a zigzag, or indeed in any other pattern you wish to create.

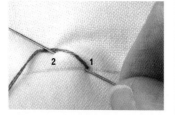

1 Bring the needle through from the back of the fabric at 1. Take the needle back through next to 1 and bring to the front at 2. With the thread passing under the needle from right to left, pull the needle through. This stitch needs to be on the slant as it is the first half of a leaf.

2 Take the needle back through at 2, stitching over the loop to secure. Bring the thread back up at 1 for the base of the next stitch.

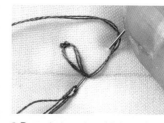

3 Repeat steps 1 and 2 to make a second loop, this time slanting it in the opposite direction.

4 This completes a single set of leaves for the flower. Bring the needle through at the bottom of the leaves and make a straight stitch upward to form the stalk of the flower.

## COLONIAL KNOT
This is a wonderful little knot for flower heads, flower centers, or anywhere where an embroidered knot is required. Here it is shown next to the lazy daisy stitches to make a flower.

1 Bring the thread through from the back to the front of the fabric at the top of the stalk of the flower. Make a loop to the right and pass the needle over the bottom of the thread and under the top, through the loop. Take the thread and wrap it over the needle. It should now look like a figure of eight.

2 Place the needle back into the fabric just next to where it came out. Before you pull the needle through, tighten the thread to form a knot. Pull the needle through to the back of the work. If desired, bring the thread from the back to the front above the first knot and repeat the above steps to make a second and third knot.

*Continues on page 32*

## SATIN STITCH

This stitch is used for outlining, filling, and shaded effects. To make the satin-stitched motif shown here, you will need to use basic satin stitch as well as long and short satin stitch.

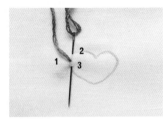

1 Draw the outline of the motif onto the fabric. Bring the needle from the back to the front on the edge of the motif at 1. With the thread to the left of the needle, take the needle back down at 2 and bring back up next to 1 at 3.

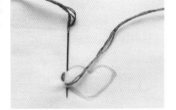

2 Repeat step 1 along the motif.

## LONG AND SHORT SATIN STITCH

If you have a large motif or you wish to shade the colors of the satin stitch, long and short satin stitch is your best option. You can use one thread throughout—single color or variegated—or two or more threads.

1 Draw the outline of the motif onto the fabric. Bring the needle from the back to the front at 1. Bringing the thread across the motif, take the needle back down at 2 and bring up about halfway back toward 1 at 3. This is a short stitch.

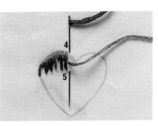

2 Take the thread up next to 4 and back down at 5. This is a long stitch. Repeat the long and short stitches until you have finished 1 motif length.

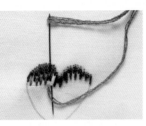

3 When you have stitched a whole row of alternating long and short stitches, work a second row of long stitches. Work enough rows to complete the motif, finishing with a row of long and short stitches. If desired, combine long and short stitches using 2 or more different threads for a shaded effect.

## SPIDER'S WEB MOTIF

This is a classic Crazy quilt stitch; embroider either whole spider's webs or corner webs.

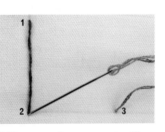

1 Choose a place on your quilt where 2 fabrics form a right angle. The right angle drawn on the fabric here illustrates this. Bring the needle from the back to the front at 1 and take back

through at 2 to make 1 long stitch along the first side. Bring the needle back out at 3 (1 and 3 should be the same distance apart as 1 and 2) then take back through at 2.

2 At equal intervals to make a fan shape, stitch 3 other long stitches in between the first 2. Start to weave a thread in and out of the long stitches, making a little stitch over the long stitch as you go to hold it in place.

3 Weave the thread across the long stitches 3 or 4 times to create a web.

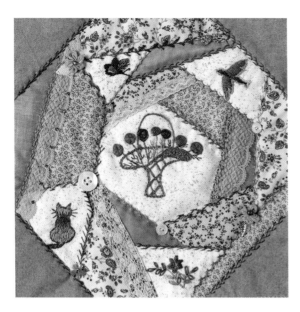

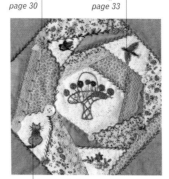

Feather
stitch,
page 30

Satin-
stitched
motif,
page 33

**THE BLOCK**
This classic Crazy block is
enhanced with satin-stitched and
other motifs in colors that
complement the chosen fabrics.

Long and short
satin stitch,
page 32

# *satin-stitched motifs*

By combining satin-stitched motifs and lace you can recreate an antique look reminiscent
of Victorian patchwork. Commercially available transfers are not always easy to find, but
with an embroidery transfer pencil and cooking parchment paper, you can create your own
patterns from any design.

## To Make This Block
### You will need
- 2 or 3 strands stranded cotton or stranded silk
- Cooking parchment paper
- Embroidery transfer pencil or No. 2 pencil
- Fabric and lace for the block
- Embellishments as required
- Embroidery hoop
- Templates (page 118)

## Transferring Motifs
When pressed, commercial transfers and
embroidery transfer pencils leave a reversed
image of a design on fabric. Many are
permanent, so check that your embroidery
covers the outlines. On light fabric, you can
trace your design with a No. 2 pencil.

## Stitching Motifs
Place your marked fabric into an embroidery
hoop and satin stitch (page 32) inside
the marked motif until you have
filled in the motif.

It is best to stitch the
motifs before using
them in a quilt
block, but they can
be added
afterward, if
necessary.

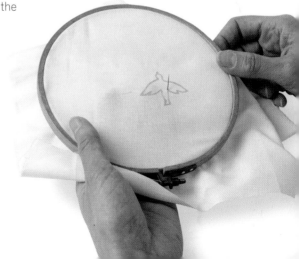

*Machine embroidery, page 35*   *Machine-sewn motif, page 35*

**THE BLOCK**

This is a Kaleidoscope block pieced from fabrics that have been embellished with machine embroidery stitches and motifs.

# *machine embroidery stitches*

The built-in stitches in your sewing machine give you tools for creating stunning quilt embellishment. Your options will vary according to your sewing machine. Experiment on scraps of fabric, and remember to make notes about any changes you make to stitch length and tension so that you can reset your machine the next time you sew.

## To Make This Block
### You will need
- Fabric, batting, and backing for your block
- Machine embroidery threads
- Metallic and standard needles
- Patterns A and B (page 122)
- Stabilizer fabric

## About the Sewing Machine
Before you start, set up your machine for embroidery stitches; refer to your manual.

## About the Threads
For machine embroidery, you can select from a variety of threads made from different fibers in a range of colors and with many different properties. Different threads will give different effects to the same stitch; see Threads (page 15). You may have to change the top tension on the machine for some threads, but always check your manual before making alterations of this nature.

## About the Needles
Some machine embroidery threads may need to be used with a special needle; for instance a metallic needle has a rounded eye so you will not snag the fibers.

## Stitching Options

Machine embroidery can be stitched just through the fabric, or it can be worked through the batting and backing as well. If you just stitch through the fabric, for instance to make a motif to be incorporated into a piece of Crazy patchwork, you will need to use a stabilizer fabric on the back to prevent puckering. This could be sew-in interfacing or a specialist product that is stitched on and then torn off.

By stitching through all the layers, or just through the top and the batting, the machine stitches act as quilting stitches and the texture created adds another dimension to the machine embroidery.

## Alternate block

Try experimenting with free-style stitches as well as using preset embroidery stitches.

# Embellishing with machine embroidery

Remember to always practice the stitch on a scrap of fabric before embellishing your block. This enables you to check that your sewing machine is set up correctly.

1 Set your machine to the required embroidery stitch. Cut out a piece of fabric 5" (12.5cm) wide and 20" (51cm) long. Draw 4 straight lines across the fabric with a ruler at 1" (2.5cm) intervals, starting 1¼" (3.2cm) from the top of the fabric.

2 Attach a piece of stabilizer fabric to the back of the fabric. Here lightweight sew-in interfacing has been used. Starting with the first embroidery stitch you have chosen, stitch along the top drawn line.

3 Stitch along the 3 other drawn lines, selecting a different machine stitch for each line.

4 Using your A template and starting from one edge of the fabric, carefully cut out 4 triangular wedges from the stitched fabric. Make sure that each triangle contains the same pattern.

5 If your sewing machine has a facility to embroider whole motifs, you can embroider motifs onto fabric and then use them within a block. Attach a piece of stabilizer fabric to the back of your chosen fabric. Embroider 4 motifs onto the fabric, leaving adequate space around the motifs. Using your template with the center cut out, carefully cut out the 4 motifs, making sure that the motif is in the center of the window. Use these triangles, those from steps 1 through 4, and 4 cut using the B template. Layer with batting and backing and quilt as desired.

**TIP**

*If you stitch the motifs onto a large piece of fabric and then cut them out it is much easier to center the design than if you cut the shapes out first and then embroider the motif.*

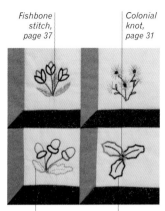

*Fishbone stitch, page 37*

*Colonial knot, page 31*

*Backstitch, page 81*

*Chain stitch, page 37*

### THE BLOCK

This is a classic Attic Window block pattern, with the addition of candlewick embroidery in the "windows." The designs represent the four seasons: spring, summer, fall, and winter, and use the most popular candlewick embroidery stitches.

# *candlewick embroidery*

This traditional type of embroidery has gained popularity again in recent years. Candlewick embroidery can be used on its own to make quilts or it can be incorporated into quilts using other techniques as added embellishment. Traditionally, candlewick embroidery was worked on muslin using special candlewick thread, either in cream or ecru. However, more modern interpretations of the technique use all kinds of threads on all sorts of fabrics, which enables you to match the color of your candlewick embroidery to the color chosen for your quilt.

### To Make This Block
**You will need**
• Pieced block, batting, and backing
• Candlewicking thread, cotton perle 8–12, silk perle, or stranded cotton (use three strands)
• Quilt or embroidery hoop
• Templates (page 119)

### About the Stitches
There are a number of basic stitches associated with this type of embroidery. They are: colonial knots (page 31), satin stitch (page 32), backstitch (page 81), stem stitch (page 37), chain stitch (page 37), and sometimes feather stitch (page 30) and fishbone stitch (page 37).

### Designs and Motifs
You can adapt both embroidery and quilting patterns for use with candlewick stitches. Look for designs that have strong outlines and areas that can be filled to add texture and detail.

To mark the design on your fabric, use a silver marking pencil or light mechanical pencil on light fabric and dressmaker's carbon or an embroidery transfer pencil on dark fabric (page 11). Carbon and embroidery transfer pencils can be permanent and so are really only suitable if you will be stitching with a fairly thick or colored thread.

Once the designs have been stitched, quilt around the edges of the motifs.

# Embellishing with candlewick embroidery

Candlewick stitches are traditionally worked through just the top layer of fabric, using a frame, and quilted afterward, but if you work them through the batting as well this helps to stop puckering and adds texture.

### STEM STITCH
This slightly slanting stitch is used for stems and outlines.

### CHAIN STITCH
This is an outline stitch or, when in rows within a drawn outline, a "filling in" stitch.

### STRAIGHT STITCH
This is a simple, single stitch that can vary in length. When sewn in sequence it can be used to make a variety of images. I have used it to make spiky flowers.

### FISHBONE STITCH
This is a good stitch for making leaves. Draw out a leaf shape and "fill in" with fishbone stitch. The stitch crosses over from side to side at an angle.

1 Bring the thread from the back to the front at 1 and take it back through at 2, slightly slanting it across the center line. Keep the thread below the needle. Bring the needle back through to the front at 3, above the thread. Position 3 should be about halfway between 1 and 2.

1 Bring the needle through from the back to the front at 1. Take the needle back through next to 1 and bring it up at 2. Making sure the thread is under the needle from right to left, bring the needle through the fabric. You should have a small looped stitch.

1 Bring the thread through to the front at 1, where the center of the flower is to be. Take a long stitch outward at 2, then take the thread through the fabric and back up a short distance away at 3.

1 Draw the outline onto the fabric. Bring the needle through from the back to the front at the top point 1. Take it back through at 2 and then bring it back through to the front at 3.

2 With the thread under the needle, take the needle back through at 4 and up at 2. Repeat this stitch along the line, keeping your stitches as even as possible.

2 Take the needle through to the back next to 2, slightly to the left, so it goes through the loop. Bring the needle back out at 3, with the thread under the needle from right to left. The stitch length between 2 and 3 should be the same as between 1 and 2. Repeat to make a continuous line of stitches.

2 Take the needle back through the center at 4 and bring back out at 5. There should be the same distance between 4 and 5 as between 1 and 2; and 4 and 5 should be the same distance apart as 2 and 3. Repeat the above steps 7 times to make 8 spikes in total (or fewer if you are making small flowers or half-flowers).

2 Take the needle through to the back at 4, just underneath point 2. Bring it back up at 5, next to point 1. Take the needle through to the back at 6, just below 4, crossing over at the center. Bring it back out at 7. Repeat this sequence, crossing over at the center each time, until you have filled in the leaf.

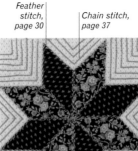

Feather stitch, page 30
Chain stitch, page 37

**THE BLOCK**
The Le Moyne Star shown here clearly illustrates the use of outline stitches to embellish blocks.

# *outline stitches*

Using a decorative outline stitch highlights the lines in a block. It can form a barrier between the colors of two adjoining fabrics, can alter the color of the fabric pieces, or can be used to give a purely decorative effect. The outline stitches can be done by hand or machine and can also be enhanced with beading.

## To Make This Quilt
**You will need**
- Pieced block, backing, and batting
- Thread
- Narrow masking tape (optional)

## About the Threads
Use any hand sewing thread mentioned on page 15 for outlining. Take care when choosing the color of the thread. If it is to provide a barrier between two adjoining fabrics, it needs to contrast but complement both fabrics. If the stitches are there to lighten or darken the color of the fabric, the thread needs to be the correct shade.

## Marking the Stitch Lines
If you are outline stitching the patches on a block, for instance the Le Moyne Star block shown here, you simply follow the seams of the patches. The stitches should fall on either side of the seam as for Crazy patchwork.

If, however, you are "echo quilting" a shape to change or enhance the color (as seen in the triangle and square patches on the block), you need to stitch in straight lines either the same space apart or evenly staggered. For straight lines you can use narrow masking tape, for instance ¼" (0.6cm), or, if you prefer, you can draw the lines with a pencil. If you are stitching by machine you can use the metal quilting guide which comes as standard with most sewing machines.

**OUTLINE STITCHES**
The illustrations at left show outline and echo stitches.

# Embellishing with outline stitches

Outline stitches can be worked through the batting as a form of quilting. This will give anything from a simple to more elaborate effect depending on the embroidery stitches you select.

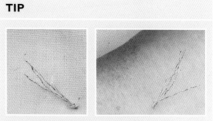

*Remember to "pop" the knot through to the batting when you start to embroider.*

1 Press your block and tack together with the batting and backing. Choose your embroidery stitch and thread. Here feather stitch (page 30) is stitched around the outline of the block with a silver thread, and a turquoise stranded cotton is used for the outline quilting on the triangles and squares.

3 Using feather stitch, embroider across all the seams of all the pieces of the star. Once you have outlined the star, "echo quilt" the squares and triangles. It is important to stitch these in straight lines. You can carefully mark the lines with a marking pencil, or, if you prefer not to draw lines on the work, use masking tape. For a small block like this, use ¼" (0.6cm) tape, placing the tape against the inner seam.

5 Move the tape and stitch on the second side.

2 Feather stitch is directional so you have to plan your stitching order. Start with a center diamond, and at its outer point feather stitch toward the center.

4 Starting from the most central part of the square or triangle, stitch along the edge of the tape so you create an inner "echo" line of stitching. Here chain stitch has been used, but you could also use quilting stitch, stem stitch, or machine stitch.

6 Move the tape and align along the line of stitches you have just made, so you create a new line of stitches that echoes the previous one. Continue echo quilting until all the triangles and squares have been completed.

Machine quilting in the ditch, page 20

Twisted insertion stitch, page 41

**THE BLOCK**
Four foundation-pieced mini-squares—or quiltlets—have been joined together using insertion stitches to make this 9" (23cm) Four Patch block.

# *insertion stitches*

This method of joining blocks together is suitable for any block that can be pieced, quilted, and backed by placing backing fabric right sides together with a block top, with batting in place, stitching around the edge, and turning inside out to finish, making a "quiltlet."

## To Make This Quilt
**You will need**
- Four quiltlets
- Stranded cotton or cotton perle No. 5 or 8
- A piece of paper slightly bigger than 2 quiltlets

## About the Thread
Use fairly thick thread for this stitch—two to four strands of either stranded cotton or cotton perle No. 5 or 8. The thread can blend in with the color of the fabric or can be contrasting.

## Working with Quiltlets
Many quiltmakers love making blocks but find that putting them together and quilting and backing them as entire quilts is daunting. With this method you can make individual "quiltlets" with either a single block pattern or a variety of sampler-type blocks and stitch them together using an insertion stitch such as the twisted insertion stitch shown on the page opposite.

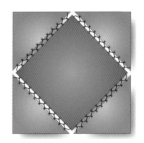

**JOINING DIFFERENT SHAPES**
Quiltlets can be made in different sizes and various geometric shapes.

# Embellishing with insertion stitches

This block is ideal for pictorial fabrics and for "framing" any special fabric or print. Insertion stitches are also well suited to candlewick embroidered squares, cross-stitched squares, and lace-centered squares.

## TWISTED INSERTION STITCH

1 Place 2 of the quiltlets next to each other and pin in place. The insertion stitch will join these 2 mini-squares together, picking up the fabric on the very edge of each quiltlet. Work from left to right. Thread your needle and "pop" the knot between the layers. Bring the needle out at the end of the bottom quiltlet. Take it through the front quiltlet's top edge.

2 Take the needle under and over the thread and then insert it at the back of the bottom quiltlet and bring through to the front at a slight angle.

3 Take the thread on the needle under and over the previous stitch and back through the top quiltlet from back to front.

4 Repeat steps 2 and 3 along the whole seam.

### TIP

*To ensure even gaps between the seams, tack the quiltlets onto a piece of paper. In the center of the paper draw 2 lines ¼" (0.6cm) apart. Tack the quiltlets in place, making sure that the edges sit on the lines. Stitch the quiltlets together; then remove the paper.*

5 To complete the Four Patch block, sew another 2 quiltlets together, and then sew the 2 new rectangles together using the twisted insertion stitch.

## HEXAGONAL BLOCK

Blocks do not have to be square. You can use this method to join other shapes, too.

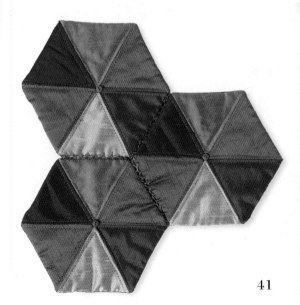

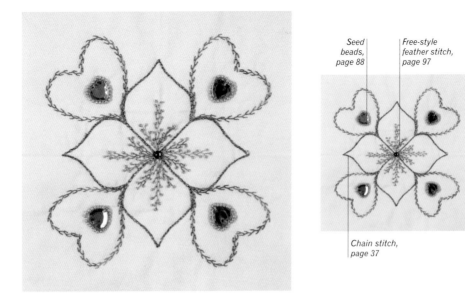

*Seed beads, page 88*

*Free-style feather stitch, page 97*

**THE BLOCK**
This block shows how embroidery and beading can enhance a simple quilting pattern.

*Chain stitch, page 37*

# *embellished quilting*

A basic pattern can be enhanced with additional embroidery and with beads. In the block shown here, heart-shaped cabochon beads, themselves outlined with seed beads, mirror the heart shape of the quilting. The stitching ties the center of the heart to the backing, and seed beads embellish the tips of the feather stitches.

## To Make This Block

**You will need**
- Plain quilt block, batting, and backing
- Quilting stencil or templates (page 120)
- Cotton perle, stranded cotton, or metallic threads
- Seed and cabochon beads

## About the Fabric

Simple plain or self-colored print fabric is best for allowing stitches to show. A soft, firmly woven fabric such as craft-weight cotton is easiest to use, but stunning effects can be achieved with silk.

## About the Threads

Choose threads that will pass through the quilt without tangling or fraying. Cotton perle or two or three strands of stranded cotton are best. Stranded metallic threads can be used as the whipping thread for a running stitch. In that stitch it does not pass through the layers of fabric and will fray less. When stitching on beads, use a fine needle and a thread that matches the bead or is invisible.

## Marking the Pattern

Choose a simple quilt pattern, one whose lines aren't too close together, from a quilting stencil, from the templates on page 120, or use one of your own design. Transfer to the fabric with a suitable marking pencil.

# Embellishing with embellished quilting

Embroidery stitches and beading can enliven your quilting. You may like to use a printed backing fabric to help mask any uneven stitches.

1 Make a "quilt sandwich" with the top fabric, batting, and backing. Starting from the center, begin to quilt along the stenciled lines using an embroidery stitch (here, chain stitch [page 37] using 2 strands of a metallic thread).

## Alternate block

This Church Dash block shows a further example of embroidery embellishment. Featured stitches are herringbone (page 29), whipped running stitch, and big-stitch quilting. The spots on the fabric used for the center are embellished with seed beads.

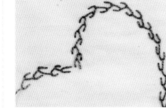

2 The outer heart shapes feature basic feather stitch (page 30). This is a directional embroidery stitch, so take this into account when starting to stitch. Here, stitches have been made one way from the center of the heart to the base, and then repeated in the other direction. This keeps all the stitches going one way (downward).

3 When you have finished the embroidery, add the beading detail to the block. Starting with the feather stitching, stitch a seed bead to the top of each feather stitch. Bring the thread through from the back at 1, remembering to "pop" the knot through to the batting.

4 Pick up a bead with the needle and pass the bead onto the thread. Take the needle back through the fabric and batting at 2. The seed bead should now be sitting on top of the feather stitch.

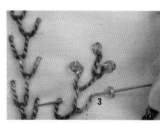

5 Bring the needle back through the fabric at the tip of the next feather stitch at 3, and apply another bead. Repeat for some or all of the tips of the feather stitches.

6 Place large cabochon beads inside the heart shapes of the embroidered quilting. Bringing

the thread through from the back, stitch through the holes on the cabochon.

7 To take away the sharp edge of the cabochon, stitch seed beads around the edge. Pick up a single bead on the needle, pass onto the thread, and then take the needle back through just behind where it came out.

8 Bring the thread back through to the front just in front of where the next bead will sit. Thread another bead and take the needle back through behind the bead. This method of stitching ensures that the beads sit close together with no gaps between them. Repeat this until you have beaded around the whole cabochon.

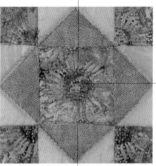

*Hand quilting stitches, page 20*

**THE BLOCK**
Embroidery and beading add definition and sparkle to the printed fabric in this block.

*Enhanced printed fabric, page 45*

*Basic feather stitch, page 30*

# *enhancing printed fabrics*

For best results, choose fabric that not only has an interesting and pleasing design, but also one that has distinct shapes or outlines that can be highlighted with stitching or beading. Threads and embellishments need to both enhance the fabric and create shape and line in the pattern.

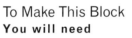

## To Make This Block
**You will need**
- Pieced block, batting, and backing
- Threads
- Beads

## Choosing Colors
The bead and thread colors need to blend in with the fabric and not overwhelm it, although some fabrics may benefit from a strongly colored thread to bring out a particular part of the design. Here metallic threads in a similar shade to the print color on the fabric are used—use stranded for hand sewing and machine thread for the machine embroidery.

## About the Stitches
Your choice of stitches will depend on the design of the printed fabric. Simple stitches that outline the main features of the fabric work well.

## Choosing a Pattern
To make the most of the pattern of the fabric in a block you need to be able to cut the pieced shapes from a particular place on the fabric. You may need to do this just once for the center or several times as in the batik Mosaic block.

Instead of block piecing, you may wish to use just one fabric cut into shapes and applied to a base fabric with fusible web and appliqué stitching.

# Embellishing printed fabrics

Make a simple block special by using fabric with an interesting design and highlighting it with embroidery and beading.

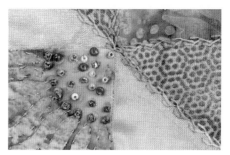

5 Repeat the beading and quilting on the corner squares, which here each represent a quarter of the center whole flower design. To complete the embellishment and to clarify the lines in the pattern, quilt the outline of the center square and the triangles with feather stitch (page 30).

1 Layer the block, batting, and backing to make a "quilt sandwich." Starting in the center, select the areas that you are going to quilt or bead. The batik print shown here has dots in the center, and so is ideal for beading and stitched knots. Using a selection of beads of different colors, either create a color pattern with them or randomly stitch them in place.

3 Outline the flower petals with small quilting stitches using 2 strands of stranded metallic thread.

4 Try changing the color for alternate petals.

## Alternate block

This block is enhanced with machine stitching. Try out threads and practice stitches on your sewing machine before embarking on a similar project. Make any adjustment necessary to tension and stitch size and note these down for future reference.

In addition to enhancing the fabric, the stitches on this block appliqué the fabric shapes to the backing fabric.

The triangle stitch enhances the fabric because it echoes the points on the diamonds, while the machine metallic thread in copper color complements the fabric. The diamond shapes are applied using the double stitch blanket stitch, and further outline quilting in satin stitch follows the line of the fabric.

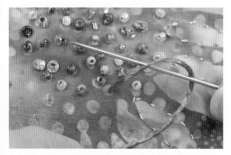

2 Add colonial knots (page 31) around the outer edge of the beading using a thick metallic thread.

# Embellishing with Ribbon and Braid

Ribbon, lace, and braids can be used for couching or covering raw edges on seams, ribbon can be used for making flowers and bows for embellishment, and lace can be placed over fabric to diffuse color or create an interesting texture. A combination of lace, ribbon, and braid can be used to weave a fabric that can be used as a centerpiece for a block pattern.

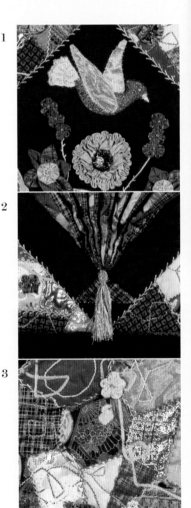

**Mikado**

*dimensions 39" (99cm) square*

The raised applied patchwork fan has been filled with an arrangement of raised appliqué flowers (1) and further enhanced with beads, sequins, and a tassel (2). The Crazy patchwork corners have been decorated with couched ribbon and braid and a selection of yo-yo flowers (3).

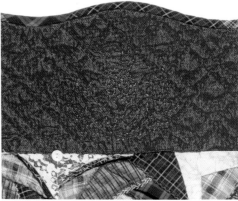

1

2

3

## Highland Fling
*dimensions 45" (114cm) square*

A quilt with a Scottish flavor made from foundation-pieced blocks that feature folded fabric corners and lace inserts. The lace (1) is meant to represent the whirling jabots of dancers and the gold pointed triangle corners represent crossed swords (2). The hand-quilted border has thistle motifs (3).

*Rosette, page 49*

*Quick piecing, page 49*

*Satin ribbon bow*

### THE BLOCK

The raw edges of the Quick Pieced Crazy Patchwork block provide an ideal opportunity to use beautiful ribbons and braids.

# *ribbons and braids*

Ribbons and braids are made from a variety of fabrics including silk, cotton, polyester, rayon, metallic, and any mixture in between. Remember to take this into account when working on your quilt as some may melt under a hot iron. If you are going to apply the ribbon or braid to a quilt, remember to make sure that it is both colorfast and washable. It is usually best to use fairly narrow ribbon—¼ inch (0.6cm) to ½ inch (1.2cm)—but this depends on the size of the piece of work. The larger the patches, the wider the ribbon they will take.

## To Make This Block

### You will need
- Foundation fabric for the block
- A selection of fabrics for the Crazy Patchwork
- Ribbons and braids

## Stitching Ribbons and Braids

Use either hand or machine stitches. If you are hand stitching you can use blind stitch (page 49) or, for added embellishment, embroidery stitches. If you decide to machine stitch try straight stitch or an embroidery stitch. Herringbone and feather stitches work well.

## Quick Piecing

Cover the seams of a Quick Pieced Crazy Patchwork block with ribbons or braids as you add fabric pieces to a base fabric. Another option is to tack all the pieces in place first and cover the raw edges afterward. When you start to apply the braid to the block, begin with the short lengths and then cover the raw edges on the ends of these with the finished sides of the longer runs of ribbon.

# Embellishing with ribbons and braids

Once your block is pieced, embroidery stitches, bows, and rosettes all add embellishment. Stitch them through the block and batting if you wish.

## QUICK PIECING

1 Cut a piece of foundation fabric the size of your finished block plus at least ½" (1.2cm) to allow for seam allowances. Decide how you will position your chosen fabric. Try to use each one at least 3 times, although this will depend on how many fabrics you are using and the block size.

2 Take the first of your fabrics. Choose one with a design that can be centered, for instance the cat in the block shown here. Cut out a piece with at least 5 sides and place it in the center with the right side facing you. Choose another fabric and cut a piece with 1 side the same length as one of those from the first piece. Place this one so that it butts up to the first, just overlapping it. Cut a strip of braid or ribbon the same length as the joining sides and place it over the join. Pin and tack in place; then stitch down.

3 Cut out a third piece of fabric that will be long enough on one side to cover the seams of 1 joined side of fabrics 1 and 2. Place it so that it just overlaps the other 2 fabrics. Place a different piece of ribbon or braid over the top of the seam. Pin and tack in place.

4 Blind stitch (see right) or embroidery stitch on each side of the ribbon or braid, or top stitch by machine. Keep adding fabric, covering the seams as you go, until you have pieced the foundation square completely.

## ROSETTES

1 Use ribbon that is about ½" (1.2cm) wide. Cut a piece 3½" (8.9cm) long. Sew a running stitch along the bottom edge. Use double thread so the thread won't break when you gather it up.

2 Gently but firmly pull up the gathers.

3 Join and stitch together the ends of the ribbon, right sides together, to form the rosette. Even out the gathers and flatten the front of the rosette. Stitch the rosette in place on the block.

## RUFFLES

Use ribbon that is ½" (1.2cm) to ¾" (1.9cm) wide. Sew a running stitch along the center of the ribbon by hand or using a sewing machine. Gather gently and use to decorate seams.

## BLIND STITCH

Bring the needle through from the back of the fabric to the front onto the braid edge and then back down directly behind this first stitch. Take the thread along the back about ⅛" (0.3cm) and repeat the stitch along the whole length of the braid.

### TIP

*Try making a double rosette by making one rosette using slightly wider ribbon and another using the ½" (1.2cm) wide ribbon, then placing the second on top of the first. For added embellishment, add a bead or sequin to the middle.*

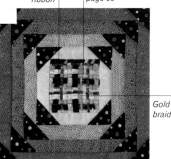

Velvet ribbon

Fabric weaving, page 50

Gold braid

**THE BLOCK**

In this foundation pieced Wild Goose Chase Log Cabin block, woven ribbons, braids, and threads form the center square.

# *weaving*

Weaving a selection of fabric strips, threads, ribbons, braids, lace, or any combination of these makes a textured and interesting center that can be used in many blocks. Choose ribbon, lace, and braid in colors to complement the fabrics in the block.

## To Make This Block
### You will need
- Block fabrics, batting, and backing
- Fabric strips, threads, ribbons, braids, lace
- Lightweight iron-on interfacing

## About the Weaving Materials
The woven center should complement the rest of the block in terms of color and size, so the smaller the woven patch, the narrower the strips need to be. The ribbons, lace, or braids also need to be washable and colorfast. Ideally the edges of fabric strips should be ironed under.

Some threads and braids are delicate and may scorch or melt under a hot iron, so use a pressing cloth on top of the weaving materials and monitor the heat.

## FABRIC WEAVING

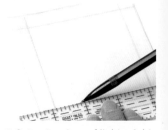

**1** Cut out a piece of lightweight iron-on interfacing the size of the finished woven piece plus a ½" (1.2cm) seam allowance all around the edge. Draw the actual stitching line onto the interfacing.

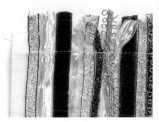

**2** Select the strips to be woven and, with the sticky side of the interfacing facing upward, start placing them along the top side (so they stretch from top to bottom), overlapping the seam at the top and bottom by at least 1" (2.5cm). Make sure that they butt up to each other with no gaps in between. Stitch them in place at the top and the bottom.

# Embellishing with weaving

Woven squares of ribbons and braids can be placed in many block patterns, either as a centerpiece or elsewhere in the block. Pieces of weaving also add texture and interest to art quilts. As an alternative to traditional weaving, try weaving through a diamond net.

3 Turn the material around 90° and repeat step 2. The ribbons should be at right angles to the first ribbons applied. This time only, stitch the strips down at the top, leaving the bottom ends free to weave.

5 Weave the first loose strip over and under the strips in turn and pull through to end.

## NET WEAVING

1 Cut out a piece of net to the size required, remembering to include a good seam allowance.

3 Continue weaving from side to side, alternating over and under, until you have covered all of the net. Place the net onto a backing fabric and stitch around the edge to secure the woven braids.

4 Using a long chunky needle such as a bodkin, cut the free end of the strip on the cross to aid threading and thread your needle with the first ribbon.

*Bodkin*

6 Weave the second strip under and over each strip in turn. Repeat until you have woven all the strips. Machine stitch along the loose ends of the strips and then on all the sides and carefully press with an iron. The strips should now be stuck down to the interfacing. The piece of woven fabric can be trimmed to the correct size and incorporated into your quilt project.

2 Choose threads, ribbons, and braids that will pass through the holes in the net easily. Using a large needle or bodkin, thread a length of ribbon and from one edge of the net start to thread over and under through the net. Choose another ribbon and thread a line over and under the net at right angles to the first row.

4 Note that the color of the backing fabric will affect the finished appearance as shown in the above examples. Trim the net to the required size, remembering to include a seam allowance. This can now be used as the center of a quilt block.

*Couching an appliqué motif, page 53*

*Machine stitched couching, page 53*

*Machine stitched couching, page 53*

**THE BLOCK**

Use couching in quilting to enhance a fabric by running a trail of couched thread across a block in curved lines, loops, or straight lines, or to cover the raw edges of an appliqué motif. The Autumn Leaves block illustrates both these uses. Couching can also enhance a printed fabric by outlining a certain area of the design.

# *couching*

Couching is a way of securing thick threads or a number of twisted threads, narrow braids, or bead trims to a piece of work. It therefore needs two threads: one thick thread to be laid across the fabric and a finer second thread to stitch the first down. These can be matching threads, or the finer second thread can be a contrasting color to add extra pattern, for instance if you are using embroidery stitches.

## To Make This Block

**You will need**

- Plain block, batting, and backing
- Threads to be couched and to use for stitching
  - Fabric to serve as source for appliqué motifs, or leaf templates (pages 118–119)
  - Fusible web

## About the Threads

Use a variety of threads and narrow braids for couching, including thick cotton perle, chainette, chenille, metallic threads and braids, wool, silk ribbon, twists of several different threads, and crochet thread.

For free-flow techniques the thread to be couched needs to be able to flow smoothly over the fabric, as couching often involves curves. Satin ribbon, for instance, is not elastic enough to create curves when being couched.

## Laying the Thread

If possible bring the thread to be couched through from the back of the fabric. If this is not possible either introduce it from the side of a piece of work or cover the raw edges by tucking them under a fabric motif or a bead embellishment.

# Embellishing with couching

Couching can be used to trail fancy threads across a block for surface decoration or to cover raw edges when applying a motif.

## CLASSIC COUCHING

1 Lay the thread to be couched onto the fabric. Bring the second thread through from the back of the work to 1 side of the couched thread. Take the needle and thread over the couched thread and put back in the work straight behind to form a vertical stitch.

2 Repeat step 1, leaving a narrow gap in between the stitches with the thread traveling on the back of the work.

## ADAPTED SINGLE STITCH CROSS STITCH COUCHING

Keep the top thread slanting the same way all along the piece of work. If you are couching a thread from left to right it's easier to have the first stitch slanting upward to the right and the second stitch that completes the stitch to the left, although it is more often seen stitched the opposite way.

1 Take the needle through from the back on the base line at 1. Take back through the fabric at 2, slanting the stitch. Bring the needle back through at 3 and back down at 4.

2 Make sure that the thread to be couched runs through the cross stitch as you work.

## HERRINGBONE STITCH COUCHING

Use the same technique as adapted single stitch cross stitch couching (left) but lengthen the stitch across the couched thread, keeping it short at the back. The stitch should fall on each side of the thread to be couched. See page 29 for herringbone stitch.

## COUCHING AN APPLIQUÉ MOTIF

You can couch a decorative thread along the raw edges of an appliqué motif.

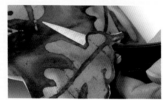

1 Select a fabric that has well-defined outlines. Press some fusible web onto the back of the fabric. When it has cooled, cut out the motif adding a scant seam allowance—about ⅛" (0.3cm) all the way around the edge. Remove the backing paper.

2 Position the motif(s) on the square of fabric that it is to be applied to and press in place. Start to apply the couching thread. Tuck the raw end under the motif by pushing it under with your needle.

3 By hand (shown here) or machine, using classic couching stitch or machine zigzag stitch, couch the thread along the raw edge of the motif.

## MACHINE STITCHED COUCHING

Some sewing machines have special presser feet for use when couching thread. You can also use a basic presser foot and guide the thread as you sew. You need to choose a stitch that covers the couched thread evenly on each side, for example a zigzag stitch adjusted to the correct width for the couched thread or, for a more decorative look, a feather stitch.

Use a machine thread that matches or contrasts with the color of the couching thread.

Inserting lace, page 55

Inserting lace, page 55

Inserting lace, page 55

**THE BLOCK**

The Fancy Fan block is based on a traditional Grandmother's Fan pattern. The inserted strips of lace enhance the look of the block, give definition to the line, and separate the individual sections. The quarter circle has a piece of lace overlaying a fabric to embellish the fabric and to diffuse the color. The seam of the base quarter circle is covered with a lace trim that hides the stitching and outlines the curve.

# *lace and ribbon*

Lace and sheer ribbon act as embellishment and also diffuse a block's color, allowing the color of the base fabric to show through without overwhelming the rest of the block. Incorporating lace into your work adds a delicate touch to any project and can soften the image of very geometric shapes.

## To Make This Block

### You will need

- Block fabric, batting, and backing
- Freezer paper
- Narrow edging lace
- Lace to cover the quarter circle

## About the Lace

Vintage lace is still quite easy to obtain from thrift stores, antique fairs, or secondhand shops and need not be expensive. However, if you need a large quantity of lace you will probably have to buy modern lace. Modern lace varies in quality and much of it is made from synthetic fibers. The cotton lace that is most widely available also tends to be thick and heavy. It is worth shopping around for really good-quality fine cotton or synthetic lace and buying it when you happen to see it. Remember also that cream or ecru will look much softer than white when put in a quilt. If you work on a large project with cotton lace, wash it in advance or it will tighten and pucker when the quilt is first washed.

## Lace Placement

Remember that lace has a right and a wrong side. The right side is the side with the even and raised thread patterns.

# Embellishing with lace and ribbon

This technique can be used with many block patterns. Try incorporating lace into a Dresden Plate block.

**INSERTING LACE: FANCY FAN BLOCK**

1 Cut out freezer-paper templates, remembering that the template's shape should appear correct on the shiny side of the freezer paper. Iron the templates to the wrong side of the fabric you are using for the fan. Cut out, adding a seam allowance. Mark the seam allowances on the back and front of the fabric. On the right side of the fabric, place the straight edge of a piece of narrow edging lace along the long side of the fan, just overlapping the seam allowance toward the raw edge. Tack in place and repeat for all 6 fan pieces.

2 Matching the seams, stitch the fan sections together but only to the length of the shortest seam (that is, to the end of the freezer paper).

3 Press the seams. Be careful, especially if you are using lace made from synthetic fibers. Tack the tops of the fans over the freezer paper and apply to the backing fabric. Once applied, remove the paper.

## Alternate block

In the alternate Windmill block, guipure trim separates the two triangle blocks, maintains the lace theme, and accentuates the "movement" of the windmill.

4 The quarter-circle base of the fan also has lace embellishment. If you use lace with a motif make sure the motif is centered on the fabric piece. Place the lace on top of the right side of the fabric, with the right side of the lace facing you. Tack the two together and trim the lace to the same size as the fabric. Treating the two as one piece, apply the quarter circle to the block.

**DIFFUSING COLOR: WINDMILL BLOCK**

1 Cut out the fabric pieces for your block. Select pieces of lace and ribbon that are an appropriate width and color when put together. Place the pieces of lace and ribbon in order along the triangle, making sure that those with finished edges overlap those without. Tack them in place and then top stitch with matching or invisible thread.

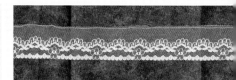

2 If you are using several different laces and ribbons, stitch the lace to each individual fabric triangle. If you are using only 2 pieces of lace and repeating them you can stitch the lace to a piece of fabric the required width and length for pattern templates. Cut the individual patches from this long strip. Start and stop with the same piece of lace. To determine the length required, make a template and count how many of these patches you need to cut from the lace fabric.

3 Lay the piece of lace along the fabric, tack, and stitch down using a short stitch.

4 Place the templates on the lace-covered fabric and cut out. The pieces are now ready to use in a block.

*Basic feather stitch, page 30*

**THE BLOCK**

The Dresden Plate block shown here has been adapted to make a Christmas Wreath block with Baltimore ruched ribbon flowers and folded ribbon leaves.

*Baltimore ruched flower, page 57*

*Ribbon leaf, page 57*

# *ribbon appliqué flowers*

Ribbon appliqué flowers are very versatile and can be used in blocks and borders or to embellish Crazy patchwork. Here the classic Baltimore ruched flower has been used to decorate a Christmas Wreath block, but the block could also be made in summer colors with flowers positioned all around the wreath to make a garland.

## To Make This Block

**You will need**

- Pieced block, batting, and backing
- Single or double-faced polyester satin ribbon, ½" (1.2cm) wide. Allow 22" (56cm) per flower. 1"- (2.5cm) wide ribbon for leaves. Allow 2" (5cm) per leaf.
- Matching thread

## About the Ribbons

Ribbon is widely available from fabric stores as well as some quilt and embroidery stores and can be bought in a variety of widths and types. Most ribbons are made from polyester and should therefore be colorfast and washable. Silk, velvet, and metallic ribbons are available (although metallic usually has polyester as its base). You may also be able to find embroidered cotton ribbon, but as this is often vintage ribbon it is not widely available.

# Embellishing with ribbon appliqué flowers

Add ribbon appliqué flowers to the quilt last. If they are added too soon, the raised parts can become squashed and misshapen. Stitch them in place in the middle, retaining the raised edges.

## BALTIMORE RUCHED FLOWERS

1 Cut the ribbon into lengths of approximately 22" (56cm). Thread up a long length of either strong single thread or double thread that matches the color of the ribbon and knot the end. Fold over 1 end of the ribbon into a right angle.

## Alternate project

For a different effect, try using lace to make appliqué flowers (pictured left). Follow the basic instructions for the ribbon leaf and join the resulting petals to make a flower.

3 Carefully pull through the thread to gather up the ribbon and make a ruched edge. Make sure that the edges are evenly gathered and then tie off the end, keeping the needle and thread in position.

2 Starting at the folded end of the ribbon, stitch in a zigzag at about 1" (2.5cm) intervals along the length of the whole ribbon. When you reach the edge, stitch over the edge. White thread is used in this photo to illustrate the stitch.

4 Next curl up the strip to make a flower. Pass the thread through the first 3 or 4 ruched "petals" and gently pull up.

5 Pull the thread so that the petals meet and make a center to the flower. Stitch in place.

6 Wrap the remaining ruching around and behind this center stitching to form the flower. Stitch in place as you go.

7 The finished flower.

## RIBBON LEAVES

Ribbon leaves can be made from any width of ribbon depending on the size of the flower.

1 Cut a length of ribbon that is twice as long as the width of the ribbon. Thread a needle with thread the same color as the ribbon.

2 Fold the 2 ends of the ribbon into the center to make a triangle with the right side facing outward. Gather along the bottom raw edge to form a leaf.

3 Stitch the leaf to the back of the flower, tucking under any raw edges.

# Embellishing with Surface Decoration

Surface decoration can include different types of stitching, quilting, beading, tassels, texturing, and manipulating fabrics—in fact, anything that is added to the surface of a quilt that enhances the appearance of the finished design.

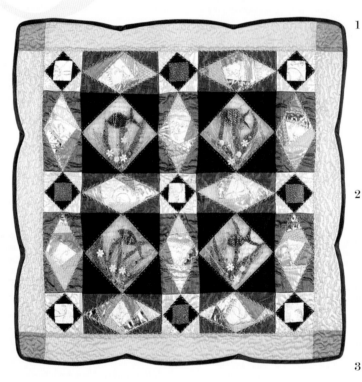

**Blue Ocean**

*dimensions 25" (63cm) square*

This little quilt is made from blue silk and silver cotton lamé along with a variety of silvery fabrics for the Crazy diamonds. The on-point center squares are made from layering an arrangement of appliqué shapes depicting fish and seaweed between voile and net (1), then stitching and further embellishing with beads and sequins. The basic quilt block Storm at Sea has been outline quilted using feather stitch (2). Free-motion quilting enhances the borders (3).

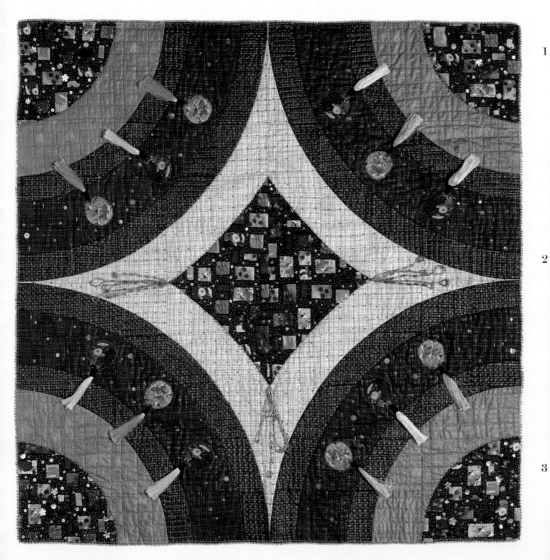

**Warding off the Evil Eye**
*dimensions 39" (99cm) square*

The circles turned outward on this quilt give the impression of an eye. Associating the quilt with the evil eye provided license to add as much embellishment and sparkle as possible, as those details were traditionally considered ways to avert the evil eye. This is an original design, hand and machine pieced, hand and machine quilted, machine and hand appliquéd (1), hand embroidered, and beaded both within the quilt and around the perimeter. It also features machine (2) and beaded (3) tassels.

*Continues on page 60*

## Windows of Opportunity

*dimensions 40" (102cm) wide x 56" (142cm) long (at its longest point)*

Windows cut from the fabric strips have been filled with Crazy patchwork made from lace and various fabrics (1). The background strips have been machine quilted with embroidered and beaded flowers (2), and seams decorated with feather stitch. Tassels add further detail (3, 4).

1

2

3

4

## One Step at a Time

*dimensions 54" (137cm) square*

A foundation-pieced quilt made from Log Cabin diamonds with Crazy patchwork centers (1). Inspired by mosaics and the undulating pavement design, this quilt has movement and sharp lines. The points of the diamonds are echoed in the border by the addition of prairie points (2). Feather-stitched outline quilting around each diamond softens the appearance of the quilt and adds surface decoration (1). The border has been seed quilted in cream to lighten the color and give a shaded appearance (2).

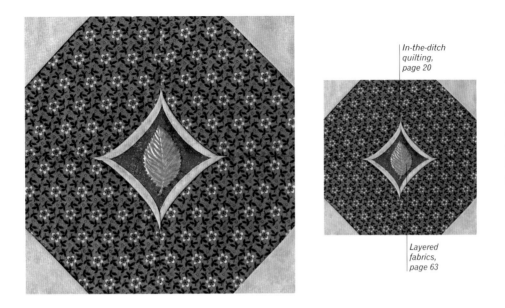

*In-the-ditch
quilting,
page 20*

*Layered
fabrics,
page 63*

**THE BLOCK**

In this original mock Cathedral Window block, folded squares of cotton fabric create a "window," which is then covered with a layer of cotton and voile with a trapped fabric leaf in between.

# *layered fabrics*

The layered fabric with the trapped motif is placed in the "window" created when the folded triangles on four squares join together. Placing the layered voile in the window and stitching it in place creates a mock Cathedral Window pattern. Choose any flat motif you like to complement your fabric and the theme of your quilt.

## To Make This Block

### You will need

- Four 5" (12.5cm) squares of main fabric
- Eight 2¾" (7cm) squares of contrasting fabric
- One 3" (7.5cm) square of window fabric
- One 3½" (8.9cm) square of voile
- Matching thread
- Fabric leaf or motif of choice
- Gluestick

## About the Fabrics

This block works best with craft-weight cotton, although you could experiment with silk for the folded triangles. To obtain sharp lines, choose contrasting colors for the base and folded squares.

## Block Placement

Use this block as a repeater block, with the triangles in the outer corners meeting the corner triangles of the adjacent blocks to create new "windows."

# Embellishing with layered fabrics

In a summery quilt use a fabric pansy or bluebell as your motif. A Western-themed quilt would be great with horseshoe charms, and an enthusiastic angler might appreciate flat plastic fish!

1 Fold each small square of contrasting fabric in half diagonally, with the wrong sides together, and press.

3 Place 2 squares together so that 2 triangles meet in the center of the block and mirror each other. Stitch the 2 squares together and then repeat for the second set of squares.

5 You will now have a block with a triangle at each corner and 4 triangles that meet in the middle, forming the window.

7 Cover the fabric square and motif with a square of voile and tack around the edges. Trim away any excess voile.

2 Place 1 of the folded triangles on 1 corner of the right side of 1 of the large squares so the raw edges align. Stitch in place along the 2 raw edges. Place a second triangle on the corner diagonally opposite and stitch in place in the same way. Repeat for the remaining 3 squares.

4 Sew the 2 sets of squares together so the 4 triangles meet to form the "window" in the middle. Make sure that the center seams and the triangles match up precisely.

6 Check the size of your 3" (7.5cm) square of window fabric against the actual window and trim as necessary to match. Take your motif and stick it onto the center of the window fabric square using a dab of gluestick.

8 Place the layered square in the "window." You may need to trim it to fit. Fold the open ends of the triangles over the raw edges of the voile in a crescent shape. Stitch down using blind stitch (page 49).

9 Stitch the required number of blocks together before quilting. Quilt around the center motif to tie the layers together.

Machine feather stitch, page 34

Lace motif, page 66

Trapping, page 65

## THE BLOCK

This Storm at Sea block has layered and trapped fabric (patches A and B), and a layer of sparkle netting (patch C). Choose your fabric colors carefully to achieve the best effect.

# *trapping*

You can "trap" almost any textile embellishment under sheer fabric as long as it does not melt when pressed. However, if you want to further embellish with surface stitching, the trapped items need to be suitable for a needle to pass through safely, so you are limited to trapping threads and fabrics.

## To Make This Block

**You will need**

- Fabric for the block
- Patterns for patches A, B, and C (page 123)
- Sheer fabric such as organza, voile, or fine chiffon
- Sparkle netting
- Fusible web
- Threads
- Sequins
- Ribbons
- Lace

## Care of the Block

You will trap threads, ribbons, and sequins between a layer of sheer fabric and a base fabric (usually cotton or silk). This method is only suitable for items that are not going to be laundered, as the bonded fabric is delicate.

## About Pressing

When pressing, make sure that you use a moderately hot iron and place a barrier, such as a heat-resistant, nonstick pressing cloth or a piece of cooking parchment paper, between the fabric and the iron. This is to protect the iron from glue and the sheer fabric from scorching or melting in excess heat. Place a second barrier on the ironing board to keep the glue from the fusible web from coming through the fabric onto the ironing board.

# Embellishing with trapping

These steps show how to prepare the fabric that you will use in foundation piecing the block. Note that if this block is to be repeated for a quilt, the triangles surrounding patch C should all be made from the same fabric (here, the darker fabric).

1 Cut out a piece of sheer fabric the size of the central square of patch A with a generous ¹/₂" (1.2cm) seam allowance. Cut out a piece of fusible web the same size. Place the sticky side of the fusible web onto the back of the sheer fabric and press the two together as directed opposite. Do not remove the paper backing.

3 When you are happy with the arrangement, remove the paper backing from the sheer fabric and place the sheer fabric on the base fabric, with the sticky side facing downward.

5 Trim any excess sheer fabric from the outer edges leaving a ¹/₂" (1.2cm) seam allowance around the edge.

2 Cut out the piece for the central square of patch A from your chosen fabric, adding a ¹/₂" (1.2cm) seam allowance. Arrange the items to be trapped on the right side of the central square fabric, well within the seam allowance. The fish shown here were cut from large sequins.

4 With a moderately hot iron and a pressing cloth on top, carefully press to bond the layers together.

6 For the central squares of patch C, cut out the required fabric and sparkle netting. The sparkle netting should be at least ¹/₄" (0.6cm) larger than the fabric patch (this allows for fraying and movement). Tack or machine zigzag stitch the two together. You can now use these as you would a single fabric. Make 4 central squares.

7 Cut out the required fabric for the long diamonds of patch B with a ¹/₂" (1.2cm) seam allowance. Cut out a piece of sheer fabric the same size. Cut out lace motifs and trap and bond them between the base fabric and the sheer fabric following the instructions for bonding patch A. Make 4.

8 Cut the remaining fabric pieces for all patches, leaving ¹/₂" (1.2cm) seam allowances. Stitch them together in an ordered sequence to finish the block (see Foundation piecing, page 16).

*Lace cut from a collar*

*Machine-stitched frame, page 67*

*Lace cut from strip*

*Purchased lace motif*

### THE BLOCK
This block was designed around the central floral motif—a modern, machine-embroidered metallic motif. It also features flowers from a wide strip of lace, small machine-made roses and butterflies, leaves from a modern lace doily, and tiny flowers from a guipure trim.

# *lace motifs*

Lace motifs can turn the simplest of blocks into elegant things of beauty. Look out for vintage lace mats and garment trims. It is always a shame to cut these up, so if possible use them as whole pieces in your work. The art is in arranging all these little gems of lace and flowers in a balanced and attractive way.

*Modern lace pattern motifs*

## About the Threads
Use monofilament thread or thread that matches the lace.

## Planning a Block
If you wish to use a medallion of lace of a specific size, then you need to plan your block around this. Think carefully about the size of your block and the pattern, including the size of the squares or motifs on the illustrated pieces. This is easier to do on an appliqué block (like the one featured above) than it is on a pieced block. Choose a simple fabric to apply the lace to, preferably one in a strong color so it shows off the lace to its best advantage.

## To Make This Block
**You will need**
- Block fabric, batting, and backing
- Lace
- Freezer paper
- Marker pencil
- Threads to match lace or monofilament

## About the Lace
Choose lace with strong patterns that can be cut out. Look for lace guipure, woven, metallic, sequined, and beaded lace, and lace motifs.

# Embellishing with lace motifs

Use lace with finished or non-fraying edges. Consider hand or machine stitching lace motifs in place through your block's batting and backing so you are quilting as you go. If you are embellishing a large quilt, sew just through the top fabric and batting. Techniques for the featured and alternate blocks are shown in the steps below.

5 Machine stitch around the marked lines. This can be done through the batting. You now have the frame. Use it as a guide for placing the lace motifs.

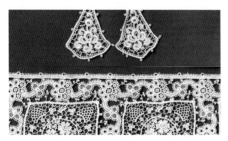

1 Select a piece of lace that is the correct size for the block you are making and check that there is enough lace to cut the required number of pieces from.

3 Carefully cut out any single motifs you wish to use.

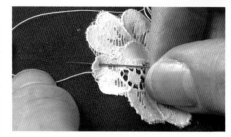

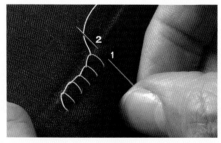

6 Once you have arranged the lace motifs in an attractive pattern, pin and tack the pieces down. Use either blanket stitch (if the edges are delicate; see instructions below) or blind stitch (page 49) to stitch the pieces in place.

2 Decide on the motifs that you wish to use from within the lace and carefully cut them out. If you make your cuts carefully you should not end up with frayed edges. You may be able to cut out square patterns as in the piece shown here.

4 To make the frame at the center of the featured block, cut an octagonal window out of freezer paper and press the template onto your fabric. Using a marker pencil, draw in the lines around the window. Mark a line ¼" (0.6cm) inside this one using a ruler.

## BLANKET STITCH

The straight edge of the stitch needs to sit on the outer edge of the lace. Bring the needle through from the back to the front on the edge of the lace at 1. Take a small stitch through the lace at 2 with the needle coming out behind the edge of the lace. The thread should be around the back of the needle.

## Alternate block

The lace for this block was taken from two small strips of vintage lace bought from a specialist shop. The central lace feature, also taken from a scrap of old lace, is made up of four motifs sewn into a pattern.

Tassels, page 68

**THE BLOCK**

The Four Patch Fancy Fan block is an ideal pattern for using tassel embellishments. The tassels have been made out of stranded cotton in colors that match the fan fabrics.

1 Select your thread. You can use just 1 thread or several different ones.

2 Cut a piece of card-weight paper the required length of your tassel plus ¼" (0.6cm). Holding 1 end of the threads against the bottom of the card, and holding the other end taut in your hand, start to wind the thread around the card.

# *tassels*

Tassels are a decorative way of finishing a quilted motif, incorporating interesting threads into the project. They can also create a deeper, luscious edge on a quilt or cushion. Simple to make, tassels can be as plain or as fancy as you wish.

## To Make This Block
**You will need**
- Block fabric, batting, and backing
- Thread
- Card-weight paper

## About the Threads
You can make a simple tassel with one thread or blend several together. You do need one thread to tie the tassel and also whip the top (see step 11 opposite), and for this it is best to choose a fine thread that doesn't fray and gives a smooth cover when wrapped around the top of the tassel. Stranded cotton or silk are good options.

## Decorative Finishes
You can also add embellishment to the tassels themselves by stitching seed beads around the top of the tassel (where you have wound the thread). You could also use a "ring" bead over the whipped part of the top of the tassel, as long as the hole in the middle is large enough to accommodate the top of the tassel. Or add a filigree cup (the kind used in jewelry).

3 Continue winding the thread carefully around the card until you reach the desired thickness. The more times you go around the card the thicker the tassel will be.

# Making a simple tassel

If you make your own tassels, you can use threads that complement your chosen fabrics or that have been used to stitch the project.

8 Pull tight, with the thread pulling downward to make the tassel head.

11 Take the needle through to the top. This thread can be used for sewing the tassel in place.

4 Choose 1 of the threads you are using for the tassel.Thread your needle with a double thread with a knot at the end. Take the needle under all the threads at the top of the tassel.

6 Carefully take the tassel off the card and with your fingers make a loop of thread around the tassel about ½" (1.2cm) down from the top of the tassel.

9 Wind most of the remaining thread on the needle around the tassel.

12 Cut through the tassel loop at the base.

5 Pull the needle just through, and then take it through the middle of the double threads and pull tight. Trap the knot under the tassel head.

7 Take your needle through the loop of thread.

10 Finish off the thread by passing it through the tassel from side to side.

13 Trim the bottom of the tassel so that the ends are straight. The tassel is complete.

*Prairie points, page 71*

*Prairie point tip stitched through to quilt back*

**THE BLOCK**
This adapted Gentleman's Fancy block is made up of triangles and squares. By adding folded triangles, you can simply and easily add texture and interest to the block.

# prairie points

Prairie points are commonly used as borders to provide either extra length or added interest. They can be used on the edge of a quilt, inside the binding, or in between the seams to add texture. They can be all the same size or of varying sizes.

## To Make This Block
### You will need
- Fabric, batting, and backing for the block
- Cotton or silk fabric for the prairie points

## About the Fabrics
Choose fabrics, such as cotton or silk, that can be easily pressed into folds with crisp edges. Try to avoid using directional fabrics because it can be difficult to keep the pattern going the same way when you are folding the material.

## About Color
Prairie points can enhance the design of a quilt through the careful use of color. They can introduce color to complement fabrics used in other parts of the quilt, or they can be used to lighten a dark fabric or subdue a bright one.

## Pattern Tips
For the prairie points for this block you need 3½" (8.9cm) squares of fabric. If you need a different sized square (the height measurement is determined by the width of the strip onto which the prairie point is to be placed) then use the following formula:

Height of the required prairie point x 2 + ½" (1.2cm) seam allowance = size of square.

70

# Embellishing with prairie points

Prairie points can be made in two different ways, each giving a slightly different appearance.

**FOLDING A PRAIRIE POINT—METHOD ONE**

1 Cut out 3½" (8.9cm) squares, 1 for each prairie point you wish to make. Fold each square in half, wrong sides together, to make a rectangle. Press.

2 Place a pin in the middle of the folded edge. Take the 2 folded corners and fold them again into the center so the edges meet. Carefully press. Repeat with all squares.

3 You will now have a triangle with 2 folded edges meeting in the center and a raw edge along the base. The right side is the side with the folds showing.

4 Place the prairie points on the piece they are to be applied to, raw edges aligned with the piece edge, right side of the piece and the prairie points facing up. Stitch the prairie points into the block seam. Note how the prairie points overlap.

5 Once the block has been completed, stitch the top points of the prairie points through to the back of the quilt as a form of quilting.

**FOLDING A PRAIRIE POINT—METHOD TWO**

1 Cut out a 3½" (8.9cm) square. Fold the square in half diagonally, with the wrong sides together to make a triangle. Press.

2 Fold the triangle in half again and press again. You will now have a triangle with 1 folded side, 1 side with raw edges, and 1 open side with 2 folded edges. Repeat steps 1 and 2 to make more prairie points.

3 Slip the prairie points inside each other so the raw edge can be placed against the raw edge of the piece they are to be applied to. Stitch into the seam.

# Embellishing with Appliqué

Appliqué can be used to add additional features to parts of a quilt. The appliqué motifs can be flat or raised, hand or machine stitched, cut out from a commercially printed fabric, or created from photographs printed on fabric.

**Christmas Eve**
*dimensions 39" (99cm) wide x 35" (89cm) long*

This is a landscape quilt, made using flat and textured piecing. The church has been printed from a photograph (note the gold fabric placed behind the windows for special effect) (1). The trees in the background have been cut from a commercial fabric (2). The poinsettias have been applied using fusible web and machine stitching (3).

1  2  3

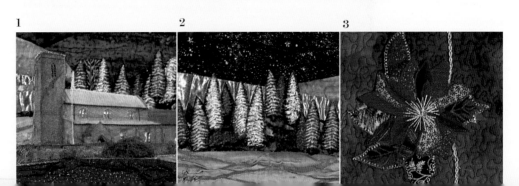

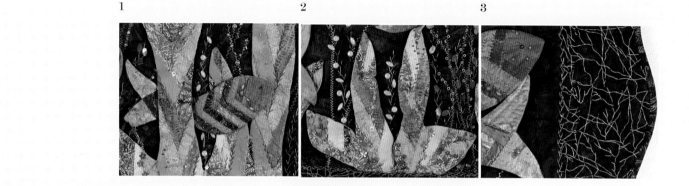

1            2            3

### Fish and Strips

*dimensions 45" (114cm) wide x 42" (107cm) long*

A basic background for the strip-pieced fish and seaweed was created from a framed panel of fabric, hand and machine stitched and embellished. Both the fish and seaweed (1, 2) have been individually strip pieced onto interfacing, quilted with embroidery, and backed to make them freestanding. They have then been partially stitched to the quilt, curving them in the process to give movement. Feather stitch embroidery frames the center of the quilt (3).

*Continues on page 74*

**Falling Leaves**

*dimensions 28" (71cm) square*

The background to this quilt is a whole piece of fabric with large leaves printed all over it. These have been outline quilted and highlighted with copper colored metallic thread (1). Individual leaves, made from Crazy patchwork and then embroidered and ruched for decorative effect (2), have been appliquéd in between.

1

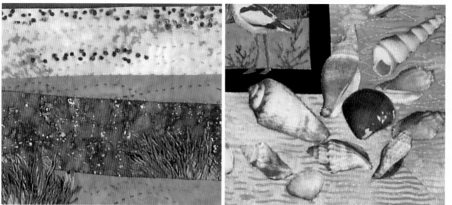

2

Shoreline
*dimensions 31" (79cm) wide x 23" (58cm) long*

A simple strip-pieced seascape, double framed and decorated with hand and machine quilting, hand embroidery (1), and bonded appliqué using photos printed onto fabric (2).

Shadow appliqué, page 77

Quilting around the appliqué motif

**THE BLOCK**
This Ocean Wave block has a shadow appliquéd anchor in the center square. Traditionally, shadow appliqué base fabric is white or cream, but this block features navy blue base fabric with a gold metallic anchor for a nautical feel.

# *shadow appliqué*

Shadow appliqué is a form of appliqué where a cut-out motif is trapped between two pieces of fabric and then outlined with hand or machine quilting. The base fabric should be a firmly woven fabric such as cotton, while the top fabric should be a sheer fabric, such as voile, chiffon, or organdy. When the project is completed the appliqué will be seen as a "shadow" through the sheer fabric.

## To Make This Block
### You will need
- Block fabric, backing, and batting
- Sheer fabric cut slightly larger than the size of the center square
- Fabric for the appliqué motif
- Fusible web
- Template (page 120)

## Fabrics
In order for the appliqué motif to show through the sheer fabric, the color of the base fabric needs to be either much lighter or much darker than the motif. Choose a sheer fabric that is as transparent as possible. Sheer fabrics come in a variety of colors and materials, and the color of a sheer fabric can be used effectively to change or diffuse the color of both the appliqué motif and the base fabric. A silver or gold metal organza will add sparkle, for instance, while a pink sheer fabric will make a white base fabric appear pale pink.

**SHADOW APPLIQUÉ**
Shadow appliqué is a nice feature for block centers.

# Embellishing with shadow appliqué

Shadow appliqué is a quick and easy way of incorporating an appliqué motif into a block without having to turn under raw edges. Try the technnique with a different block pattern and perhaps a floral motif.

1 Cut out the pieces of fabric for the center square. You will need a square of base fabric, a piece of sheer fabric, fabric for the appliqué motif, and fusible web.

3 Place the sticky side of the fusible web onto the back of the motif fabric and carefully press. If you are using a delicate fabric, use a pressing cloth between the iron and the fusible web. The gold fabric shown here is black on the back.

5 Remove the backing paper from the motif and place the anchor in the center of the base fabric square.

7 Place the sheer fabric on top of the motif. Using a fine needle, tack the fabric in place, but be careful not to stitch through the motif. Make up the block with the layered square in the middle. Remove the tacking.

2 Using a pencil, trace the anchor motif onto the paper side of the fusible web.

4 When the fabric has cooled, carefully cut out the motif.

6 With a pressing cloth between the iron and the fabric, press the anchor motif in place.

8 Tack the block, batting, and backing together. Quilt around the outside edge of the appliqué motif. This will "trap" the motif in place and add definition to the design. Quilt the remaining block as required.

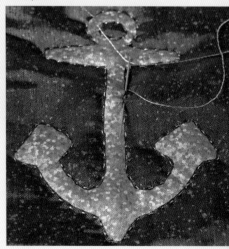

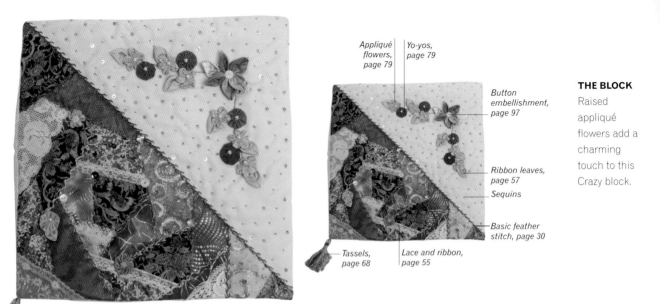

*Appliqué flowers, page 79*

*Yo-yos, page 79*

*Button embellishment, page 97*

*Ribbon leaves, page 57*

*Sequins*

*Basic feather stitch, page 30*

*Tassels, page 68*

*Lace and ribbon, page 55*

**THE BLOCK**
Raised appliqué flowers add a charming touch to this Crazy block.

# *raised appliqué flowers*

Raised appliqué flowers and foliage always add an extra dimension to a quilt whether used in a block, a border, or indeed as a single embellishment on a piece of Crazy patchwork. Appliqué flowers can be made from a variety of fabrics and colors that complement the piece of work, can be made in different sizes to suit your project, and are particularly useful for adding extra color or sparkle.

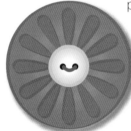

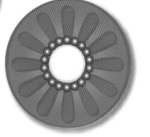

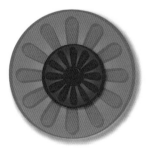

**ADDING EMBELLISHMENTS**
Fabric flowers can be embellished with a bead stitched in the center, or different-sized buttons, or a circle of seed beads.

## To Make This Block
### You will need
- Pieced block, batting, and backing
- Fabric for the flowers
- Beads or tiny buttons

## Selecting Fabrics
This technique for making flowers is based on gathering small circles of fabric: these are known as "yo-yos." Choose fairly fine fabrics and lace that are not prone to fraying, in colors and textures that complement your block.

# Embellishing with appliqué flowers

Appliqué flowers can be useful for covering up any slight imperfections. If you find that you have an unhappy join or seam when piecing a block, try embellishing to enhance your work and hide the error at the same time.

### MAKING YO-YOS

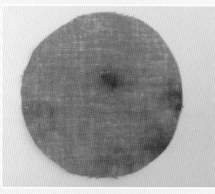

1 Cut a circle of fabric twice the finished diameter plus ½" (1.2cm). That is, for a 1" (2.5cm) finished size, cut a circle 2½" (6.3cm).

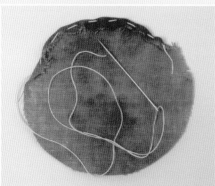

2 With the wrong sides together, fold in a tiny hem of a scant ¼" (0.6cm) all around the edge. Using a strong thread or a double thread, turn a series of gathering stitches as you fold.

3 When the circle of stitches is complete, pull the thread tightly to gather up the fabric. Make the opening as small as possible by pulling the gathers closely. Take the thread through to the back and finish off thread securely. The right side is the gathered side.

4 To finish, when applying the yo-yo to your piece of work, place a bead or tiny button in the center and a ribbon leaf (page 57) underneath.

### MAKING FABRIC FLOWERS FROM YO-YOS

1 Follow steps 1 through 3 for making yo-yos. Visually, divide the flower into 5 or 6 equal sections. Take the thread through the middle of the flower, around the side at the edge of 1 section, and back through the middle. Pull tight.

2 Repeat a little way along for the next section. A petal will have formed. Repeat for remaining sections. Stitch a bead or button to the center as required.

### USING TWO FABRICS

To make a pansy, stitch 2 strips of fabric together, 1 purple and 1 yellow. Cut out a circle from this and follow steps 1 through 3 for making yo-yos. Continue as for a fabric flower, but make 3 sections, 2 narrow and 1 wide.

Flat appliqué, page 81

Foundation piecing, page 16

**THE BLOCK**

This foundation-pieced Flower block has been enhanced by adding a simple appliquéd butterfly motif.

## *flat appliqué*

Use flat appliqué as a form of embellishment on patchwork patterns. The curved shapes created in appliqué will soften the geometric lines of pieced blocks and add extra detail and interest.

### To Make This Block

**You will need**

- Pieced block
- Fabric for the appliqué pieces
- Templates (page 120)
- Lightweight iron-on interfacing
- Embroidery and quilting threads

### About the Stitches

The following are useful stitches for appliqué:

**Blind stitch** (page 49) for hand-sewn appliqué

**Blanket stitch** (page 67) for hand-sewn or machine appliqué. Often used for raw edges and bonded motifs

**Satin stitch** (page 32) for hand-sewn or machine appliqué

**Stem stitch** (page 37) for hand-sewn features such as flower stems and antennae

**Colonial knots** (page 31) for hand-sewn features such as flower centers, eyes, and antennae

It is important that you do not press the appliqué pieces during the preparation process.

1 Draw the appliqué shapes (for the butterfly, 2 taller hearts and 1 wider heart) on the non-adhesive side of the interfacing. Draw all the pieces that will be cut from the same fabric in 1 row, leaving room for a seam allowance around the edge of each motif.

2 Place the strip of interfacing on the piece of fabric you have chosen for the motifs, with the adhesive side facing the right side of the fabric. Stitch along the drawn line of each appliqué

# Embellishing with flat appliqué

Appliqué can be stitched either by hand or machine using a variety of methods. Here the butterfly motif has been applied using a blend of modern (iron-on interfacing) and traditional (hand stitching) techniques.

shape, using a short machine stitch or by hand using backstitch (page 81). Note that to make the iridescent set of butterfly wings a sheer fabric was layered over a base fabric.

3 Cut out the motifs leaving a small seam allowance of ⅛" (0.3cm). Clip the curved edges, cutting through the seam allowance perpendicular to the line of stitching but not cutting through the stitching.

4 Cut a small slit in the center of the back of the interfacing, just large enough to turn the fabric through. Turn all the pieces

inside out. The adhesive side of the interfacing should now be on the back. Ease out the edges with a point turner but do not press.

5 Using the picture as a guide, build up the pieces on your pieced block to make the motif. When you are happy with the arrangement, press with a warm iron. (If you are using a sheer fabric, protect the surface with a pressing cloth.) The back of the motif will now be stuck to the pieced block.

6 Stitch the motif in place by machine or by hand using blind stitch (page 49).

7 To create the body section of the butterfly use satin stitch (page 32) by hand or machine. If using a machine, you will need to have a variable-width satin stitch. Start with a very narrow stitch and gradually increase the width toward the center of the butterfly, and then decrease the width as you approach the other end.

8 To finish, stem stitch (page 37) the antennae and add a colonial knot (page 31) for each tip.

## Backstitch

Backstitch is useful for making flat appliqué pieces and for many basic quilting techniques.

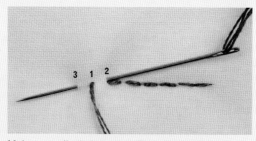

Make a small stitch to start. Then take the needle through at 1. Take a small stitch behind and through the fabric at 2, and then bring the needle through at 3. The length of stitch 1–2 should be the same as the length of stitch 2–3. Repeat this sequence for the required distance, keeping stitches as even as possible.

*Machine satin stitching*

*Curve created by thick and thin Log Cabin pattern*

*Broderie Perse (page 83) in wreath shape*

**THE BLOCK**

This foundation pieced thick and thin Log Cabin block uses cream fabric for one side of the log cabin and patterned fabric for the other side. The cream sides (thick logs) form the center of the block onto which the Broderie Perse is applied.

# *broderie perse*

Broderie Perse is a form of appliqué where motifs, often flowers and leaves, are cut out from printed fabrics and are arranged and stitched onto a background fabric. The motifs can be cut from one single fabric or from a number of different fabrics to build up a pattern.

## To Make This Block
### You will need
- Pieced block, batting, and backing
- Fabrics with flower and leaf motifs
- Fusible web
- Threads to match or complement the fabrics
- Seed beads

## Traditional Appliqué
Following the traditional method, the motifs for Broderie Perse are cut out with a seam allowance, which is then turned under when applied to the base fabric. If you use this method, leave a ¼" (0.6cm) seam allowance and appliqué the motifs using needle-turn appliqué and blind stitch (page 49).

## Bonded Appliqué
In bonded appliqué (shown here), fusible web is placed on the back of the floral fabric before the motifs are cut out. The motifs can then be cut with a tiny seam allowance, pressed in place, and the raw edges embroidered with either machine or hand stitches. The best machine stitches to use are zigzag, satin

stitch, or blanket stitch. The best hand stitches are blanket stitch (page 67), chain stitch (page 37), or satin stitch (page 32).

If your fabric is fairly firmly woven and does not have a tendency to fray, you can use stitches that do not cover the edges completely (blanket stitch or zigzag stitch). If your fabrics are fine and may fray, use a stitch that covers the edges completely (satin stitch or chain stitch). Here satin stitch has been used.

## Quilt As-You-Go
To stabilize your work, minimize puckering, and quilt the Broderie Perse, you can embroider the edges through the batting. The beading can then be done through the patchwork, batting, and backing to tie the layers together.

# Embellishing with Broderie Perse

The colors chosen for the motifs complement the colors in the block and have been taken from two different fabrics. The block has been finished by adding seed beads and long stitch to the center of the flowers.

1 Select the motifs that you wish to use from your chosen fabric(s). If they are widely spread out across the fabric, cut them out leaving a good seam allowance around all the edges.

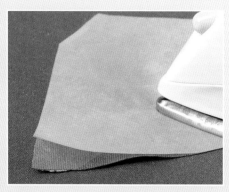

2 With an iron, press fusible web onto the back of the fabric motifs. Allow to cool.

3 Cut the motifs out, adding a tiny seam allowance of about 1/8" (0.3cm).

4 Peel off the fusible web's backing paper.

5 Place the motif onto the block, positioning as desired. Carefully press in place.

6 Layer the block with the batting. Stitch around the raw edges of the motifs by machine or hand.

7 Layer the backing with the block and batting. Finish the flower by adding beading and stitch detail.

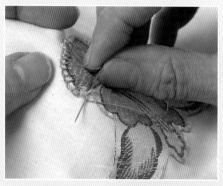

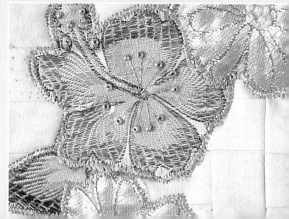

# Embellishing with Treasures

The quilts in this gallery are decorated with a variety of special embellishments to enhance their design. These decorative features can be old or new and include buttons and beads, sequins, shisha mirrors, charms, and shells.

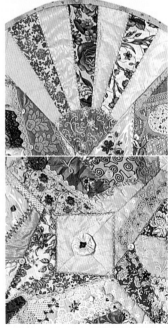

**Hidden Depths**
*dimensions 60" (152cm) wide x 75" (190cm) long*

A Crazy quilt (1) made in squares and set on point with a fan feature edging (2). Made using a variety of different fabrics—cotton, silk, lace, and blends of these—in pale pinks, green, and cream, and embellished with embroidery, beads, buttons, sequins, and appliqué flowers (3).

**Time and Tide**

*dimensions 34" (86cm) wide x 45" (114cm) long (at its longest)*

This is a modern-style Crazy quilt. The fabrics represent the changing colors of the sea and sand, and decorative hand embroidery (1), prairie points (2), sequins, beads (3), and shells (4) embellish.

*Continues on page 86*

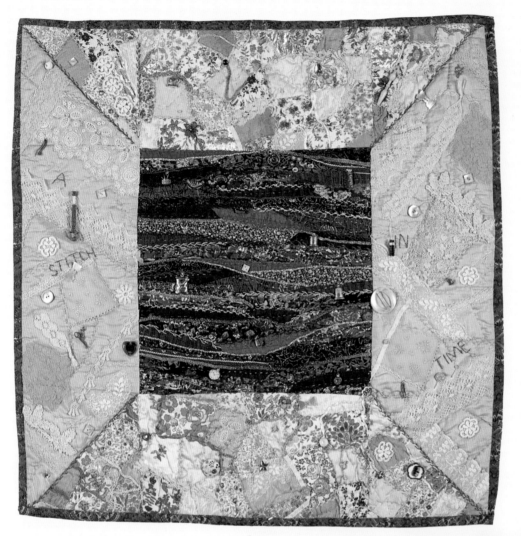

## A Stitch in Time
*dimensions 24" (61cm) square*

A miniature quilt that celebrates the beauty of lace old and new as well as offering a showcase for a collection of needlework-themed embellishments: old buttons, buckles, modern charms (1), and tiny lace bobbins. The center of the quilt has been strip pieced with texture to bring to mind the center of a spool of thread (2).

1

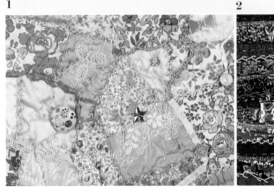

2

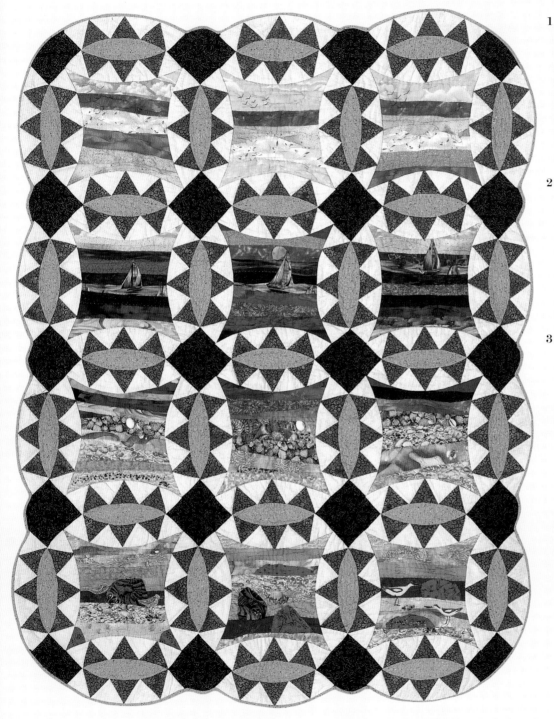

1

2

3

**Postcards of Home**
*dimensions 38" (96cm) wide x 50" (127cm) long*

A double wedding ring–style design where the center circles are made from small seascapes. The quilt is strip pieced and textured with quilted and embroidered details (1, 2). The shell fabric has been enhanced with additional padding from behind with shells stitched to the surface (3).

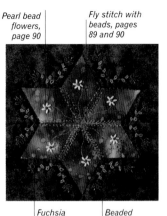

Pearl bead flowers, page 90

Fly stitch with beads, pages 89 and 90

Fuchsia flower, page 90

Beaded leaves, page 91

## THE BLOCK

This Six-Point Star block is richly embellished with beads. Make the block using either the traditional English hand-pieced-over-paper method or sew partly by machine using freezer-paper templates, which means you have to stitch only the outside edges to the block by hand.

# *seed beads*

Beads can be used to add color, sparkle, and decorative features to quilt blocks. Available in many different sizes, colors, and types, they can be used to embellish embroidery stitches, make beaded motifs, or enhance a fabric.

## To Make This Block

### You will need
- A pieced block, batting, and backing
- Complementary threads or clear nylon thread
- Seed beads, long pearl beads, and bugle beads

## About the Fabrics

Mottled and marbled fabrics are ideal for this block as they clearly display the embroidery and beading. The beading designs are the "stars of the show," so it is important that they are not overwhelmed by strong patterns.

## About the Threads

The threads need to complement the fabrics chosen. Here two strands of stranded cotton and two strands of stranded metallic thread are used for embroidery.

Use either clear nylon thread or polyester thread in a color that matches the bead. You could also use a good-quality metallic thread if color matching is difficult, but this is not quite as strong or durable.

## About the Beads

As the beads are being used to embellish embroidery stitches and to make motifs on a patchwork block, they need to be washable and colorfast. The color of the beads needs to complement your chosen fabric. Here we have used a selection of glass seed beads (some with an opaque finish and some with a clear finish), bugle beads for the flowers and on the fly stitch, and small long pearls and metallic beads for the flowers on the diamonds.

# Embellishing the block

The block is quilted and embellished with a combination of hand embroidery and beading. The embroidery, if stitched through all layers of the quilt "sandwich," will also quilt the block.

## Stitching Options

Seed bead embellishment can be done through just the top two layers (the block and the batting), or through the backing as well when the beading is used as a form of quilting. However, if you take it through all three layers it can look untidy on the back unless you are very careful to "pop" all the knots through to the back and only stitch through the top two layers for some of the work.

**BEADED STITCHES**
Seed beads add shine to embroidery.

**FLY STITCH**
This stitch, which is worked vertically, is stitched on the diamonds so that it falls centrally along the seam.

1 Bring the thread through from the back to the front of the fabric at 1. Take the thread through to the back at 2.

2 Bring the thread back through to the front at 3. This should be halfway between 1 and 2. Pass the thread under the needle.

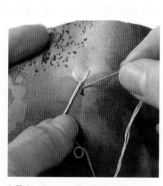

3 Take the needle through to the back, making a short vertical stitch at 4. This makes a single fly stitch (as used for the birds in the sky).

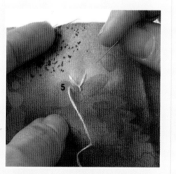

4 Bring the needle back to the front at 5, a little way down from 1.

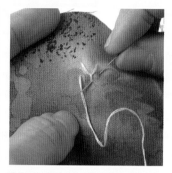

5 Repeat steps 1 to 3 to make a second stitch.

6 Continue until you have reached the end of your required line of stitches.

*Continues on page 90*

## STITCHING ON A SINGLE SEED BEAD

Remember to use a fine needle and strong fine thread when attaching the beads.

1 Bring the needle through to the front of the fabric where the bead is to be positioned ("pop" the knot through the batting) and pick up a bead.

2 Take the needle back through in between the fabric and the batting and bring to the front where the next bead is to be placed. If there is a long distance between the beads, backstitch before moving on to the next bead.

## MAKING A PEARL FLOWER

Make sure that you allow for the length of the bead when taking the needle back through the fabric so that the bead sits flat.

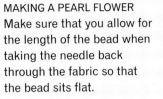

1 Draw the outline of the flower onto your fabric either freehand with a marker pencil or with an outline and dressmaker's carbon.

2 Stitch the flower stem using stem stitch (page 37).

3 Using the method for stitching a single seed bead, stitch the pearl beads on in a circle, always coming back to the center point.

4 Sew a single bead in the center of the pearl beads.

5 The completed flower.

## MAKING A FUCHSIA FLOWER

The basis of the beaded loops that make the flower head and leaves is lazy daisy stitch (page 31), but instead of just thread the stitch is made from threaded beads.

1 Mark a stem line on the fabric.

2 Embroider the stems using stem stitch.

3 Make the flower with three loops. Make the center loop first. Bring the thread through from the back at 1. Thread 12 beads.

4 Take the needle to the back at 1 and to the front at 2, taking the thread and beads under the needle with an equal number of beads on each side.

5 Take a small stitch over the thread at 3. Take the needle through to the back and bring to the front at a point next to 1. This will make the center looped petal.

6 Repeat this process to make 2 more looped petals, 1 pointing out at an angle on each side of the center looped petal. Bring the needle back to the top between the center loop and the right-hand loop, thread a bugle bead and then a seed bead, and take the needle to the back. Repeat between the center loop and the left-hand loop. Take the needle to the back and finish off.

7 Make the leaves using the same method as for the flower loops but using 6 green beads.

FAST FREEZER-PAPER PIECING
Try this freezer-paper method for a quicker, simpler way to make your Six Point Star block.

1 Cut out freezer-paper templates for the diamonds and iron to the back of your fabric. Cut out, adding a 1/4" (0.6cm) seam allowance.

2 Carefully matching the seams and the points on the freezer paper, sew the diamonds together in sets of 3 to make half a star. Stitch by hand or machine.

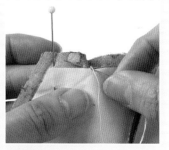

**NOTE:** Stitch to the end of the freezer paper (stitching toward the outer edge of the star).

3 Carefully matching the center and each end, stitch the 2 halves together to make a 6-point star.

4 Tack the outer fabric over the papers to finish the edges. Stitch the star to a square of fabric using blind stitch (page 49), removing the papers as you go.

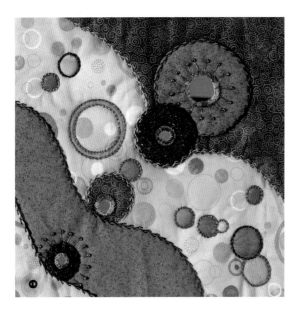

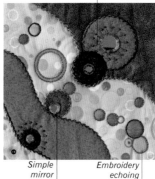

*Mirror stitching decorated with beads, page 93*

*Simple mirror stitching, page 93*

*Embroidery echoing mirror shape*

### THE BLOCK

This modern, curved block uses fabric printed with circles to illustrate the use of shisha mirrors. The block shows the application of different-sized mirrors and different ways of decorating them within the work. The patchwork has been further embellished with embroidery and embroidered quilting.

# *mirrors*

Traditional mirrors, known as shisha, are made from glass, and you can use them to embellish all sorts of quilted items, from cushions and quilts to bags and jackets. Shisha has been used for centuries in folk art embroidery in Asia, India, and Russia, as well as in traditional embroidery and stump work (raised embroidery) in England.

## To Make This Block
### You will need
- A pieced block, backing, and batting
- Shisha mirrors
- Firm thread to sew on the mirrors

## About the Mirrors
Buy shisha mirrors from fabric or craft stores in different-sized circles as well as other geometric shapes. It is also possible to buy plastic shisha mirrors, which often come with prestitched edging.

## About the Threads
You need to use fairly firm thread to stitch on the shisha mirrors. Cotton, silk perle, or three strands of stranded cotton are all suitable.

## Working with Mirrors
Shisha mirrors are usually made from glass, so take care as they have sharp edges and may break or chip.

The traditional glass shisha mirrors have to be attached by stitching a framework of embroidery around the edge of the mirror. You can use blanket stitch (page 67), buttonhole stitch (page 95), or a twisted buttonhole stitch. Once the shisha mirror is firmly fixed in place you can embellish it with extra embroidery stitches or beading around the edge.

# Embellishing with mirrors

Shisha mirrors add sparkle and interest to a design. They work especially well on quilts or blocks with design features in the same shape as the mirrors (often circles, but sometimes in other shapes too).

1 Place the mirror in position on your work. If you find it difficult to hold the mirror in place, put a dab of white glue behind the mirror, leaving it to adhere before you start to sew. Thread a needle with a colored thread that complements the fabric. Bring the needle through from the back to the front of the fabric at 1 and take back through at 2.

2 Bring the thread back through to the front at 3 and take back down at 4.

3 Work around the mirror until you have made four "bars" of thread—two which go vertically across the mirror, and two which go horizontally down the mirror. Note that the last thread should pass under the first one.

4 Repeat steps 1 to 3, starting farther around the mirror, so that you have a second grid diagonally across the first. This forms the basic framework for the stitches. You are now ready to stitch the mirror in place.

5 Try blanket stitch, buttonhole stitch, or twisted buttonhole stitch. These are like the latter. Bring the thread from the back to the front of the fabric at the edge of the mirror. Take the working thread over a framework thread and the needle under and back over a framework thread and the working thread. Pull through.

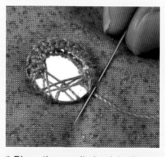

6 Place the needle back in the fabric at the edge of the mirror and take a tiny stitch with the thread under the needle where it came out.

## Alternate quilt

The mirrors on this quilt echo the shape of the round appliquéd motifs.

7 Repeat steps 5 and 6 until you have sewn around the whole mirror.

8 Decorate the mirrors with beads or additional embroidery.

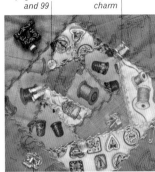

Using buttons, pages 97 and 99

Metal spool charm

Sewing machine charm

**THE BLOCK**
This simple little Crazy block celebrates all things to do with stitching, combining sewing-themed fabrics and charms.

# charms

Charms are small trinkets, usually made from either metal, silver plate, silver, gold, brass, glass, ceramics, or plastic. Don't forget that charms don't have to have been originally made for that specific use, and many interesting trinkets can be reclaimed from old jewelry and other decorative items found at yard sales and thrift stores.

## To Make This Block
**You will need**
- Pieced block, batting, and backing
- Charms
- Narrow ribbon

## Attaching Charms
If you want to attach the charms with invisible stitching, use thread that matches the charms or invisible thread. If you want to feature the stitching, use thread that complements the block.

To use charms to tie the layers of a quilt together, stitch them to the quilt through all the quilt layers. Otherwise, stitch them to the top layer only.

## About the Charms
Many quilt shops, embroidery shops, or bead shops sell charms produced especially for the quilt market. They come in many different styles and can add detail to a piece of embroidery. A butterfly or bumblebee charm could hover over embroidered flowers, and a selection of shell charms could embellish a beach scene. Not all charms should be laundered.

# Embellishing with charms

Like all forms of embellishment, charms should complement your block in terms of color and style. Apply them sympathetically.

## OVERSEWING
Oversewing is the simplest method for attaching charms.

1 Take the thread from the back to the front at 1. Then take the needle through the loop on the charm. Take the needle back through the fabric next to 1, passing the thread over the charm as you go.

2 Bring the needle back through to the front, passing through the charm. Hold the thread to the left. Repeat until the charm is firmly fastened. Tie off the thread.

## Charms on display

The charms at left give an idea of the great range available for purchase and collection.

## BUTTONHOLE STITCH
Buttonhole stitch is strong. It's ideal for use with metal charms that may rub against the thread over time.

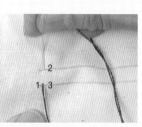

1 Take needle through from the back at 1, back through at 2, and up again at 3, making sure that the thread passes under the needle from left to right.

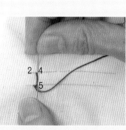

2 Take the needle back through at 4 (next to 2), and back up at 5, with the thread passing under the needle from left to right. Repeat.

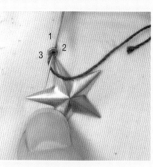

3 When attaching a charm you won't, of course, be stitching in a straight line but around the loop. The needle will come up through from the back of the fabric and through the loop on the charm at 1. Pass the needle back down behind the loop of the charm at 2, and then up and back through the loop at 3 with the thread passing underneath the needle from left to right.

## TYING WITH RIBBON
You can tie charms in place using narrow ribbon. Stitch the bows down once they are tied so that they don't come undone and cause the charms to fall off. You can also stitch charms in place with seed beads, a bead holding the loop in place. Refer to the instructions for sewing on a button with seed beads on page 99.

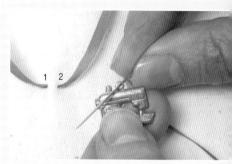

1 Cut a piece of narrow ⅛" (0.3cm) silk or synthetic embroidery ribbon about 10" (25cm) long. Starting from the front (1), take the ribbon through to the back. Leaving half the length at the front, bring the needle back through 2 next to 1. Then pass the needle through the loop of the charm.

2 Take the needle away and tie a reef knot: place right ribbon over left and tie, then left ribbon over right and tie. Finish with a bow.

Wood button
Plastic button
Ceramic bead
Metallic button

**THE BLOCK**
This foundation-pieced block has been designed specifically for this collection of buttons. The buttons used are a mixed selection—ceramic, wooden, metal, and plastic—and are arranged on the block to form a picture. They provide a decorative and novel finish to the block.

# *novelty buttons*

Buttons come in all shapes and sizes, from traditional round buttons made from plastic, wood, ceramics, or shell to the many themed buttons depicting everything from flowers to birds to lighthouses.

## To Make This Block
**You will need**
- Pieced block, batting, and backing
- Buttons
- Thread

## About the Buttons
Buttons can be purchased from quilt stores, quilt shows, and specialist suppliers. They can also be recycled from clothing gleaned from thrift stores.

## About the Threads
The buttons can be stitched on using thread that matches the buttons, so that it is as invisible as possible, or using decorative thread that becomes part of the embellishment process.

# Embellishing with novelty buttons

The right group of novelty buttons will add a really cheery touch to your block. Stitch through the quilt top, batting, and backing if you want to use the buttons to tie your quilt.

### ADDING BUTTONS

Select several buttons with a garden theme and arrange them on your foundation-pieced block in a manner that creates a garden scene (or choose another theme). Stitch them to the block with invisible or matching thread.

### EMBROIDERING FOLIAGE

Free-style feather stitch is used to make the foliage. Unlike basic feather stitch (page 30) where you try to keep the stitches of even length, free-style feather stitch requires stitches that are uneven.

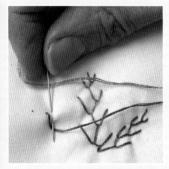

1 To make the foliage, start with small free-style feather stitches at the top and gradually make them longer as you move down.

2 Work the stitches from side to side as for basic feather stitch.

3 Stitch at least 3 trails of feather stitch, all meeting near the base.

4 When you have finished the embroidery, stitch on button leaves.

## Alternate block

This second block is more traditional—a flower appliquéd to a background using bonded appliqué and feather and blanket stitches. The centers of the flowers are made from buttons stitched on with beads. The tiny bee is from a theme pack of buttons.

### STITCHING ON A BUTTON WITH A TIE

For a decorative feature or to add detail to a tied quilt, stitch buttons on with tied thread.

When you start stitching on a button, leave 5" of thread on the top of the work. When the button is secure, bring the needle to the top of the work, unthread it, and tie the remaining thread and the 5" length in a reef knot in the center of the holes on the button.

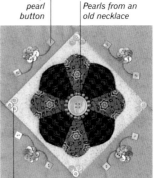

Square mother-of-pearl button

Pearls from an old necklace

Old shirt buttons

### THE BLOCK
This block is a simple, small Dresden plate, set on point. It is a traditional block, decorated with modern mother-of-pearl buttons in different shapes and sizes as well as some beads taken from an old broken string of pearls.

# antique buttons and beads

Old treasures are special in some way. They may have sentimental value, for example your grandmother's old bead necklace, or they may be collectible, such as antique buttons. They are special additions that need to be shown off within a piece of work, so both the fabric and design of the block should complement the antique buttons or beads.

## To Make This Block
### You will need
- Pieced block, batting, and backing
- Antique buttons and beads
- Seed beads

## About the Buttons and Beads
There is no single source for these special treasures: some may come from family and friends; some from antique shops and yard sales; some from stalls at quilt shows; and some from specialist stores. If you love embellishments and you buy them when you find something special, then you will build up your own collection.

## Attaching Buttons and Beads
Stitch buttons through the top, batting, and backing of your block. Sew small, round pearl buttons to create flowers with a bead at the center. A large button surrounded by pearl beads makes a nice feature for the center of a block.

# Embellishing with antique buttons and beads

Old buttons and beads can make wonderful additions to quilt blocks either individually or when made into motifs or stitched in a special design.

## SEWING ON A BUTTON WITH SEED BEADS

1 Bring the needle up from the back to the front of the fabric and through 1 of the button's holes.

2 Pick up a seed bead with the tip of the needle. Make sure that the seed bead is larger than the hole in the button. It can be the same color as the button or a contrasting color.

3 Take the needle back through the hole in the button that you came up through. The seed bead should sit in the buttonhole.

4 Take the needle back through to the front through a second hole in the button, pick up a seed bead, and repeat step 3. Repeat for the remaining 2 holes.

5 The finished button.

## CREATING A FLOWER FROM BUTTONS

1 Select small, thin buttons that are the same size. Here 7 small shell buttons have been chosen.

2 Stitch a button securely to the fabric and bring the needle back through the hole that is nearest to the next button to be sewn on. Put the next button in position, slightly overlapping the one before, and take the thread down through the first hole in the new button. In the photo, this has been repeated 3 times.

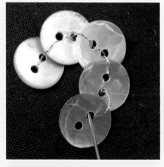

3 Bring the thread back through the same hole and take back down through the second hole in the new button. Take it back up again through the same hole, ready for the next button. Put the next button in position, slightly overlapping the one before, and take the thread down through the first hole in the new button (fifth button in photograph).

4 Repeat the above steps until all the buttons have been sewn on, remembering that odd numbers look best. Bring the thread through to the center of the flower and stitch a bead in place. Here a pearl bead has been used to match the shell buttons.

5 The finished flower.

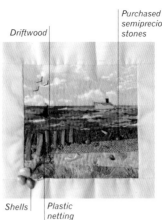

*Driftwood*

*Purchased semiprecious stones*

*Shells*   *Plastic netting*

**THE BLOCK**

This foundation-pieced pictorial block features a seashore scene. The finer details have been added using appliqué, embroidery, and found object embellishment.

# *found objects*

You can make embellishments from a variety of everyday objects including driftwood, feathers, and silk flowers. Even the netting used to package fruit can be used to decorate your quilt or wall hanging. So use your imagination when adding embellishments to your projects.

## To Make This Block

### You will need

- Pieced block from fabrics that represent the sky, sea, and sand
- Pictorial fabric with boats
- Threads that complement the fabric
- White glue
- Fusible web
- Shells (buy them predrilled or attach your own with glue)
- Wood (tree bark, driftwood, or twigs)
- Pebbles or tiny, predrilled, semiprecious stones
- Seed beads
- Plastic netting

## Use Caution

Embellishments like these are unsuitable for use on anything that children might have access to as there is a choking risk.

> **TECHNIQUE TIP**
>
> *For an extra bit of decoration, use the seed bead method for applying a button (page 99) to stitch the predrilled stones to the block.*

# Embellishing with found objects

Remember that these slightly unusual embellishments are not usually washable and are therefore only suitable for wall hangings and pictures.

1 Using fusible web, appliqué any details such as boat fabric motifs to the pieced block. Layer the block top, batting, and backing and baste the layers.

2 Quilt the sea, sky, and sand with wavy lines in colored thread that matches the background.

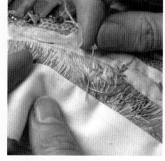

3 Using free-style feather stitch motifs (page 97), embroider the sand dunes in the bottom section (this can also be done after adding embellishments).

4 Stitch the seed beads along the shoreline to create coarse gravel. Make sure that these are not stitched where the breakwaters are to be placed (see block picture as a guide). Stitch predrilled shells and larger predrilled stones in place.

5 Carefully break off or cut some strips from a thin piece of driftwood, bark, or twig to make the breakwaters. Using the picture and pattern as a guide, stick the pieces in place, with the longest breakwater at the front.

6 Cut out a piece of netting and scrunch it up. This netting was from the packaging around oranges and is made from plastic so it will not fray.

7 Stitch the netting in place alongside the breakwaters.

8 Apply a light covering of white glue to the back of the undrilled pebbles and shells and leave to set slightly before positioning them on the block.

9 Finally, stick a few large shells in the bottom corner of 1 side of the block so they are just falling onto the outer border. Leave to dry flat before using the block in a project.

# Embellishing with Art Media

Art quilts seem to lend themselves to using a varied and unusual collection of embellishment techniques and offer great freedom for self expression and experimentation. Try enriching your quilts with computer-printed images, painting and printing, foiling, texturing, and crayon transfer.

**Beachcombing**
*dimensions 40" (102cm) wide x 62" (157cm) long*

Inspired by North Norfolk, England, this seascape has been pieced with textured foundation piecing (1) using commercial and hand-painted fabrics, embroidered, and embellished with beads, driftwood, dried seaweed, photographs on fabric, and shells (2).

1

2

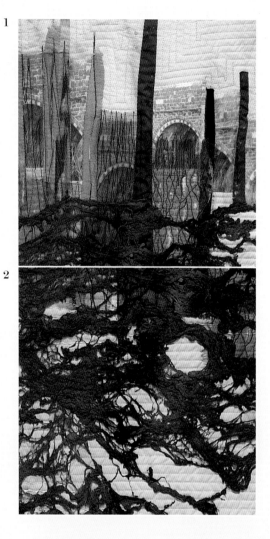

**Autumn Bridges**

*dimensions 39" (99cm) long x 18" (46cm) wide*

A wholecloth quilt, tea-dyed and machine quilted. A photograph of a single bridge arch was changed to a sepia format, resized, and then printed on silk and cotton (1). Cotton, silk, and organza strips were appliquéd, giving the feel of rushes (1). Dyed raw silk was boiled repeatedly and hand appliquéd to represent autumn debris (2).

*Continues on page 104*

## Floodline

*dimensions 39" (99cm) long x 22" (56cm) wide*

Hand-dyed cotton sateen appliquéd with cotton and silk strips (1) to represent the neatly piled debris after autumn floods. Machine quilting with very short and very long stitches is emphasized with black beading (2) applied in a meandering curve down the quilt. Machine-quilted willow leaves (3) frame the top.

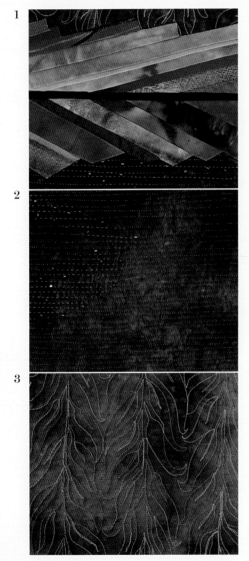

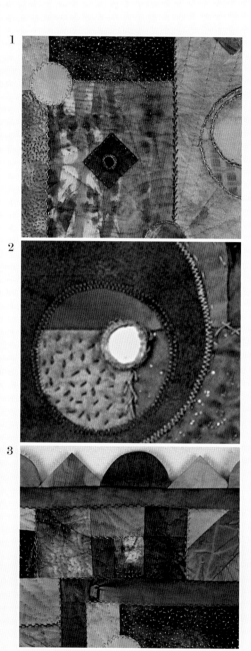

**Sparkling Symmetry**

*dimensions 35" (89cm) wide x 45" (114cm) long*

Most of the fabric for this quilt was colored using fabric paints (1). Some of the blocks have been made from fabrics that have had glittery pieces bonded and trapped beneath a layer of voile. Appliqué circles have been bonded to the pieced background, which has then been embroidered and quilted using a variety of stitches and threads and embellished with mirrors (2). The half circles and triangles along the quilt's edges give added interest (3).

*Gold foil*  |  *Copper foil*

*Hand quilting, page 20*

## THE BLOCK

A traditional Pumpkin Seed quilt pattern has been enhanced by the addition of a special foil that can be applied to fabric using either fusible web or flexible glue. Quilting done with a variety of threads and stitches adds a lovely finish.

# *foil*

Foil adds a special element to your work. Carefully choose certain areas of your work to "gild" with foil to highlight aspects of a design, add interest to a simple pattern, or give a lustrous appearance to your finished project.

## To Make This Block

### You will need

- Block fabric, batting, and backing
- Threads
- Soft pencil
- Metallic foil in gold and copper
- Fusible web or flexible glue as specified by the foil manufacturer
- Fine beaded trim in gold
- Pressing sheet
- Quilting stencil

## About the Foils

Purchase special fabric foils from mail-order suppliers and quilt and stitching shows. Foil can be purchased in a variety of metallic colors, some of which provide special effects. Although they are designed to be washable at low temperatures, it is not advisable to use foils on items that need frequent laundering. They are therefore best used when making wall hangings or bags.

## Working with Foils

Always refer to the manufacturer's instructions for the method they recommend using—either applying fusible web or a flexible glue that dries clear—with their particular brand of foil.

Working with foil requires a little practice, so before applying it to your project try it out on a piece of scrap fabric.

Take care when applying the fusible web and foil; the products get hot when pressed.

# Embellishing with foil

Remember that these slightly unusual embellishments aren't highly washable and are therefore only suitable for wall hangings and other items that don't require frequent washing.

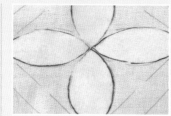

1 Using a soft pencil, lightly draw a quilting design on a 10" (25cm) square of fabric. The square can be trimmed to 9½" (24cm) once completed, but the extra fabric will compensate for fraying when working. Use a stencil if you wish, making sure that the design is centered on the fabric. Do not use a pencil or pen that will become permanent when heat is applied.

3 Place the fusible web cutouts in position on the fabric. Press in place with a warm iron, but do not remove the backing paper.

5 Cut out a piece of foil that is slightly larger than the area you are about to cover. Here copper foil has been used for part of the center square and gold foil has been used everywhere else. Place the foil on top of the fusible web with the right side (metallic side) of the foil facing up.

8 The metallic side of the foil will bond to the surface of the fabric and the clear base paper will come away.

6 Cover the foil with a pressing sheet and press with a warm iron until the foil is stuck to the fusible web. Leave to cool. Repeat steps 4–6 with the remaining areas to be gilded, only removing the paper backing from the fusible web that you are working on. Make sure that the iron does not touch the areas that have already had the foil applied.

2 If your foil manufacturer recommends the use of fusible web, trace the outlines of the areas to be "gilded" onto fusible web. Cut them out. If your foil manufacturer recommends the glue method, follow the manufacturer's instructions instead of steps 2–8 here.

4 Remove the backing paper from the area of fusible web that you are ready to apply foil to. Leave the other backing on until you are ready to apply the foil to those parts. Note that if the iron is placed on an area that has already had the foil or fusible web applied to it, the foil or fusible web will be removed by the heat of the iron.

7 When the foil is cool, carefully peel it away. Note that if you remove the paper before it is cool then the metallic surface will come away too.

9 Once the foil has been applied to the desired areas, layer the square, batting, and backing to make a "quilt sandwich" and start to quilt the design. Here chain stitch (page 37) has been used around the center square with couched beaded trim around the outer edge of the center square. The curved, gilded motifs are outline quilted with chain stitch, with the remaining lines quilted using classic quilting stitch. The center has been whipstitched through a running stitch with metallic thread to echo the effect of the foil.

*Free-style feather stitch, page 97*

*Foundation piecing, page 16*

*Shell photographs*

*Pekingese photograph*

## THE BLOCK

This simple Beach Hut block has a foundation-pieced center framed with a pieced, mitered border. The block has been embellished with appliquéd photographic images of shells and a little dog, which have been printed on special fabric.

# *photographic images*

Many people enjoy making quilts to commemorate a special occasion, and incorporating photographs into a quilt is a lovely way to do this. You can put family photographs on fabric and use them for the center of blocks, or bond images taken from the natural world (trees, flowers, shells, birds) to the quilt as appliqué motifs.

## To Make This Block

**You will need**

• Pieced block, batting, and backing
• Threads
• Images to transfer
• Printer fabric
• Fusible web

## About the Printer

If you have an "all in one" inkjet printer that photocopies, scans, and prints straight from the computer, you can use any of your own drawings or photographs as well as any copyright-free images you have access to. This means that as well as digital images you can use printed photographs and artwork. These images can either be photocopied straight onto the fabric or scanned into the computer first and then printed onto the fabric.

When printing, always use good-quality ink cartridges, and print using the most appropriate quality setting on your printer for the weight of fabric. You may need to experiment to get the best results.

## About the Fabric

Purchase fabric to use in your printer from specialist suppliers or quilt stores. It comes with a paper backing, which you remove once you have printed the image. Alternatively, you can buy a product to treat fabric with. If you need to transfer a small number of images it is best to use the paper-backed fabric. You can purchase sheets of it in a variety of fabrics and finishes, including cotton, fusible cotton, linen, and silk. Make sure that you choose a product that is washable once the color has been set if this is necessary for your project.

## Printing Efficiently

First run a test sheet using normal paper to check that the image prints with the color and size as you want it. Next place the paper-backed fabric sheet in the paper tray—which way up depends on how your printer feeds the paper through. Print straight from the computer or photocopy the image to be reproduced onto the fabric. Remember that you can combine a selection of images on a piece of paper and then photocopy them to maximize the whole sheet of fabric.

Finish the fabric following the manufacturer's instructions. This usually includes pressing with an iron to set the color.

> **TIP**
>
> *Use details from photographs of landscapes or seascapes to embellish your quilt. An appliqué of a flower bed or stone wall would add warmth to a domestic scene.*

# Embellishing with photographs

Try using photographs of people, pets, landscapes, seascapes, or special features in this block. These can then be further enhanced by embroidery and quilting.

1 Prepare the printer fabric following the manufacturer's instructions. Print the images onto the fabric (see opposite), finish following the manufacturer's instructions, and remove the backing paper. Attach a piece of fusible web to the back of the fabric and cut out the chosen images. Remove the backing paper.

2 Arrange the printed fabric pieces on your block. With a medium-hot iron, press the chosen images onto the base fabric to bond them together. Make a "quilt sandwich" from the block, batting, and backing. Quilt the picture as desired.

3 Machine stitch around the bonded photographic images using machine zigzag stitch and a thread that is either invisible or matches the images.

4 Embroider the beach grass on the sand dunes using free-style feather stitch (page 97) and add other details as required.

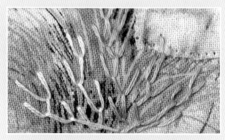

5 The embroidery enhances the photograph.

*Bonded heart shapes, page 121*

*Dimensional paint covering raw edges, page 111*

## THE BLOCK

This appliqué block illustrates the use of dimensional fabric paint. The raw edges of the appliqué motifs are covered with gold fabric paint and the block is quilted by hand on the outside edge of the paint.

# *dimensional fabric paints*

Dimensional fabric paint is a glue-like substance that dries to reveal sparkle and color. It is applied to fabric rather like icing is used to decorate a cake and can be used to embellish any block by creating whirls, letters, and dots—in fact, any shape that you can draw.

## To Make This Block

### You will need

- Fusible web
- Fabric for the base square and hearts
- Heart template (page 121)
- Gold dimensional fabric paint
- Batting and backing

*Experimenting with paint flow*

## About the Dimensional Paint

There are different brands of dimensional fabric paint and they require slightly different techniques. It is therefore important to read the manufacturer's instructions before use.

## Pattern Detail

This is a simple heart filigree pattern. The smaller hearts are the cut-out centers of the larger hearts.

# Embellishing with dimensional paints

Dimensional paint is a quick and fun way to add surface decoration to your quilt project and is most suited for use on wall hangings, bags, and art quilts.

1 Draw the filigree heart pattern on the fusible web 4 times. Place the fusible web on the back of a piece of your chosen heart fabric and press. Leave to cool.

2 Carefully cut out the hearts on both the inner and outer lines. Remove the paper backing.

3 Cut a 9½" (24cm) square of base fabric. Fold in half twice to make a smaller square, then fold again diagonally. Press then open to reveal 8 positioning lines. Put the hearts on the backing fabric, using the pressed lines and picture as a guide to placement.

4 Press the hearts in place.

5 Place the block on a firm, flat surface to cool. Shake the bottle or tube of paint. Gently squeeze the paint onto a piece of scrap fabric until it comes out in an even line. Apply the paint to the outside edges of all the hearts so it forms even lines around the appliqué images, covering the raw edges. This takes a little practice so you may want to experiment on scrap fabric first.

6 Leave the paint to dry. The paint will look milky when applied, but will gradually clear as it dries and the gold will shine through.

7 Layer the block with the batting and backing. Quilt around the design either inside or outside the dimensional paint.

Basic feather stitch, page 30

Colonial knot, page 31

Crayon transfer, page 113

Chain stitch, page 37

### THE BLOCK

This basic On-Point Square block is ideal for use as a pattern for quilted or appliqué embellishment. Fabric crayons have been used to print the picture of a poppy in the middle of the center square.

# *fabric crayons*

Fabric crayons look and feel rather like wax crayons. They come in a variety of colors and you can shade and blend them together. After you use transfer fabric crayons to color an image onto paper, you can iron the image onto fabric. The image is therefore reversed.

## To Make This Block

**You will need**

- Block fabric, batting, and backing
- Poppy template (page121)
- Pressing cloth
- Transfer crayons
- Transfer paper (cooking

## About Fabric Crayons

There are a number of brands of fabric crayon, and they perform differently. Some fabric crayons work best on fabric that has some synthetic fiber content such as polyester and cotton, while others will work on most fabrics. It is therefore important to read the individual instructions on the different brands of crayons to ensure the best results.

## Using Fabric Crayons

Use fabric crayons to color the image on paper first. Transfer the image to the fabric using a medium-hot iron. Press the fabric further once the image has transferred, to fix the color, and then wash the fabric to check for colorfastness and to soften the fabric. Always follow the instructions on the crayon package.

Place a pressing cloth under the fabric. This stops the image from marking your ironing board. Place a second pressing cloth on top of the transfer paper to protect the iron. Place the fabric between two pieces of clean paper when pressing to set the color.

## Quilting This Block

Stitch the embroidery through all the layers of the block—the top, batting, and backing—or just through the top two.

## Making a Drawing or Rubbing

You can draw your own image or use rubbings, for instance rubbings from embossed wooden blocks.

To make your own image, take a piece of paper and draw the outline of the picture you wish to color. If you do not want your image to be reversed when transferred, color on the back of the drawing. Outline the shapes in a dark shade of the color to be used—here the poppy has been outlined in dark red— then color in using a lighter shade. Color in the lighter parts first—shade the red of the poppy and then add the black center detail last.

To make your own rubbing, secure the paper in place over the rubbing and rub backward and forward to color as evenly as possible. Cut out the part of the image you wish to transfer. Blow or shake any bits of crayon off the paper so they are not transferred to the fabric when pressed.

# Embellishing with fabric crayons

Try your crayons on a small piece of fabric to see the individual effect before embarking on the whole pattern.

1 Using a pencil, draw an image on your transfer paper.

2 Using the transfer crayons, outline the picture and then color it in as required. Shade the lighter areas first, and then the darker ones. Shake off any loose pieces of crayon.

3 Take the piece of fabric for the center square and place it right

side up on a piece of paper on your pressing board. Place the colored transfer on the fabric with the crayon side down. Tape or pin in place. Place a pressing cloth or piece of paper on top to protect your iron. Avoiding the pins or tape, and using a medium- or low-temperature iron depending on the type of fabric you are using, press the image in place. You usually need to hold the iron in place for at least 1 minute, but check the instructions for your crayons.

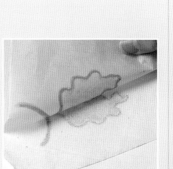

4 Carefully lift 1 corner to see if the image has been transferred successfully. If not, repeat the pressing process.

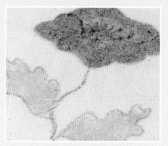

5 When the image has been transferred, remove the transfer. Place the fabric between 2 pieces of paper and press again to remove any excess color and to fix the image. Wash in warm or cold water (depending on the manufacturer's instructions) to check for colorfastness.

6 Use the fabric in a pieced block. Layer the block, batting, and backing. Outline quilt the block and add details to the image. Chain stitch (page 37) around the flower and leaves. Make the stamens using long stitch and add a colonial knot (page 31) to the top of the stamens. Embroider along the seams of the square using feather stitch (page 30).

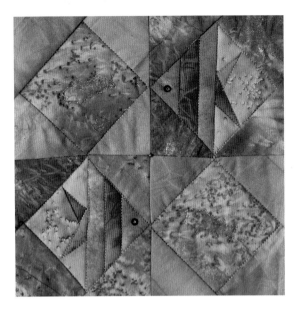

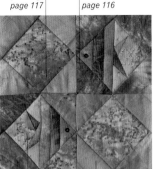

*Simple printing, page 117*

*Multicolors, page 116*

*Salt effect, page 115*

*Multicolors, page 116*

## THE BLOCK

This foundation-pieced Fish block shows off the beauty of the painted fabric. One of the advantages of painting your own fabric is that you can create it specifically for your project, so approach it creatively.

# *fabric paints*

Painting your own fabric creates a unique piece of work from which you can make quilts or other projects. Try painting the fabric with a basic color and then decorating it with additional paint finishes, printed images, painted images, or salt effects. Once stitched, you can further embellish the quilt block with embroidery, quilting, and beading.

## To Make This Block

### You will need

- Fabric, backing, batting
  - Fabric paints
  - Brushes and foam brushes
  - Disposable gloves
  - Blending palette
  - Disposable pots for mixing and water
  - Plastic frame
  - Plastic bags (ideally sealable)
- Plastic spoons
- Rock salt
- Printing blocks or stamps

## About Fabric Paints

Recently the performance and diversity of fabric paints has improved. The most common kinds of paint are transparent, opaque, metallic, and pearlescent.

Transparent paints give the effect of watercolor paints. They can be mixed together to produce different colors or diluted to lighten the color.

Opaque paints have a thicker consistency than transparent paints and the colors are stronger. They can be mixed together or diluted and are ideal for use with printing blocks.

Metallic paints can be diluted and brushed over the surface of fabric to give a shimmery effect or used with printing blocks or paintbrushes to create a pattern.

Pearlescent paints give fabric a sheen.

## About Colors

To start, buy paint in primary colors: red, yellow, and blue. You will also need black, white, and silver or gold metallic paint. Using just these six paints you will be able to mix a variety of colors. Yellow and blue make green, of course. Yellow and red make orange, and if you add a dab of black and white you get sand color. Experiment!

## About Fabrics

Natural fibers such as cotton, linen, or silk are best to use for fabric painting. If using cotton cloth, choose one that is prepared for dyeing or prewash your fabric to remove any dressing in the cloth.

## Getting Started

- Cut your cloth into manageable pieces that fit your work area/frame.
- Soak your fabric and wring it out well (you can work on dry fabric if you prefer).
- Cover your work area with a protective covering of plastic.
- Put up a drying line that is just for the painted fabric, and put down plastic in an area for flat drying.

## Fabric Care

Once your painted fabric has dried, press it to fix the color following the paint manufacturer's instructions. Then wash the fabric at hand-hot temperature to check that it is colorfast and to soften it.

# Embellishing with fabric paints

Fabric paint will behave differently depending on the type of fabric it is being applied to, how diluted the paint is, whether you work on wet or dry fabric, and how it is dried. It is therefore important to make sure that you paint enough fabric for your project at one time.

**SALT EFFECT**

1 In a plastic pot mix enough paint to cover your fabric. Use a ratio of 2 spoonfuls of paint to 1 spoonful of water.

3 Place the fabric on a piece of paper and lay both on a flat drying area. While the paint is still wet, sprinkle the fabric with rock salt.

2 Place wet (but well wrung out) fabric in the frame. Using a foam brush and long sweeping movements, paint the cloth from side to side and then from top to bottom to avoid evident brushstrokes.

4 Leave the fabric to dry and then brush off any excess salt. The salt creates a wonderful effect on the fabric.

*Continues on page 116*

## ADDING SHIMMER

1 Prepare your fabric as for salt effect (page 115), stopping after step 2.

2 Mix up some metallic paint. Use a ratio of 2 spoonfuls of paint to 1 spoonful of water.

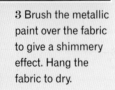

3 Brush the metallic paint over the fabric to give a shimmery effect. Hang the fabric to dry.

## MULTICOLORS

1 Mix up 3 or 4 different colors of paint including tints of the primary colors (made by adding white). Place the wet, wrung-out fabric in your frame. Brush a very diluted shade of your chosen base color across the fabric using a foam brush.

2 Using a foam brush, place spots of the different colors evenly all over the fabric.

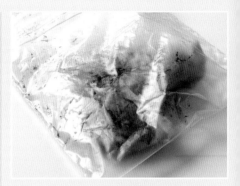

3 Place the fabric in a plastic bag. Seal the top and squeeze the bag to spread the paint across and through the fabric.

4 If you want to, add a little undiluted gold and/or silver metallic paint to the bag and squeeze again. Remove the fabric from the bag and hang it out to dry. The result is a subtle blend of colors (below).

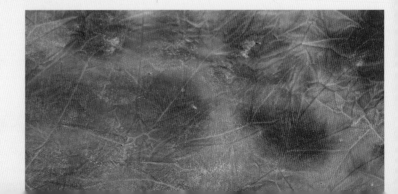

## SIMPLE PRINTING

To give more detail to your dry painted fabric, add a pattern using printing blocks or stamps.

## MIX AND MATCH

You can combine these techniques for even more effects. Paint a fabric one color, place it in a plastic bag and add a metallic paint, squeeze, and dry. Add salt to any combination and dry the fabric flat. Fold painted fabric and dab paint into the folds, place the fabric in a plastic bag, scrunch a bit, leave for half an hour, unfold, and dry!

1 Place the fabric on a firm, flat surface. Paint the printing block or stamp with opaque or metallic fabric paint—enough to transfer the design but not so much that it will smudge. Practice printing on a piece of scrap fabric.

2 Print the design onto the fabric by placing the stamp firmly on the fabric and pressing down. Remove the stamp. Dry and set the color with a hot iron.

### SAFETY

- *Always read the manufacturer's instructions and follow the safety advice.*
- *Work in a well-ventilated room.*
- *Wear protective gloves; the paints will stain hands and nails very easily.*
- *Have a set of pots, brushes, utensils, and salt for use with paints only.*
- *Never eat or drink in the area that you use for fabric painting.*
- *Dispose of leftover paint and paint water in a drain other than the kitchen sink.*

# Alternate Block

This Freestyle Flower block started with the soft multicolored fabric with touches of sparkle, painted using the multicolors method (page 116). The handpainted purple and green fabrics complement the multicolored fabric.

A flower stamp and a dragonfly stamp decorate the green fabric.

This simple block is machine pieced and quilted to highlight the fabric. Pink lazy daisy flowers, seed quilting on the center block, embroidery stitches along the seams, and beading add beauty and sparkle.

To try seed quilting, add small, straight stitches to the surface of your block. The stitches should be placed densely and should face in random directions.

# Templates

The motif templates and patterns on these pages will help you make several of the blocks in the Techniques section.

## Motif templates

**PAGE 33 SATIN-STITCHED MOTIFS**

Embroider these motifs in satin stitch and other stitches of your choice.

**PAGE 52 COUCHING**

Use these templates to cut leaves from any fabric for use in the couching block.

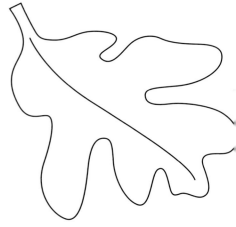

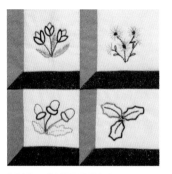

**PAGE 36 CANDLEWICK
EMBROIDERY MOTIFS**

These motifs provide embellishment for the block on page 36.

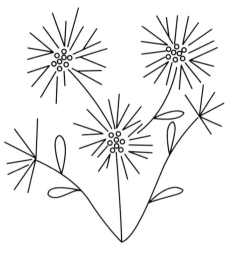

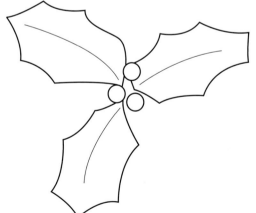

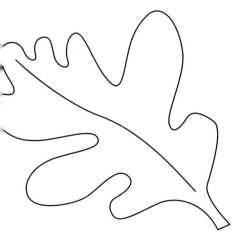

*Continues on page 120*

**PAGE 42 EMBELLISHED QUILTING**

Use these templates to guide your embellished quilting.

**PAGE 76 SHADOW APPLIQUÉ**

Cut out this anchor in fabric and fusible web to embellish the shadow appliqué block.

**PAGE 80 FLAT APPLIQUÉ**

These heart shapes form the butterfly on the flat appliqué block.

**PAGE 110 DIMENSIONAL FABRIC PAINTS**

The nested heart shapes above are the pattern for the appliqué motifs shown on page 110.

**PAGE 112 FABRIC CRAYONS**

Trace and color this poppy with fabric crayons to recreate the block on page 112. The image will be reversed when transferred, so color on the back of the traced image.

*Continues on page 122*

# Pattern piece templates

**PAGE 34 MACHINE EMBROIDERY STITCHES**

Templates A and B will help you cut the pieces for the block on page 34.

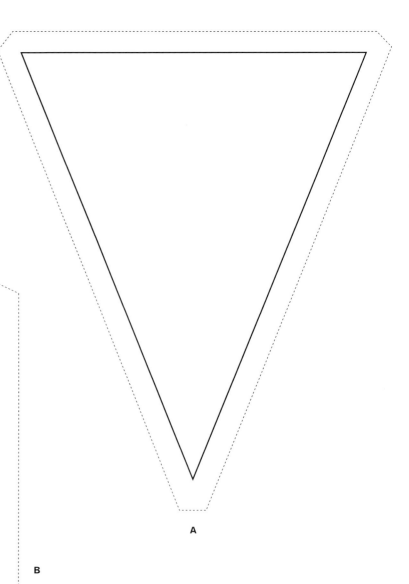

A

B

A

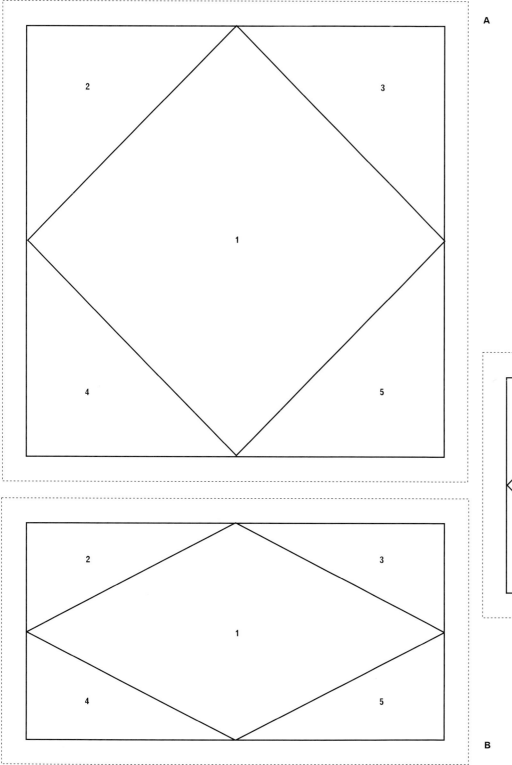

**PAGE 64 TRAPPING**

Follow the order given on these templates when foundation piecing patches for the block on page 64. Once all the patches are foundation pieced, join them together to make the block.

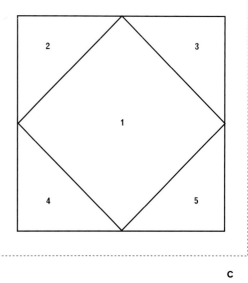

C

B

**Albers, J.**
**INTERACTION OF COLOR**
(New Haven, CT: Yale University Press, 1971)
A classic text on the subject of color.

**Beyer, J.**
**PATCHWORK PATTERNS**
(McLean, VA: EPM Publications, 1979)
Basic pattern drafting of traditional blocks.

**Brackman, B.**
**ENCYCLOPEDIA OF PIECED
QUILT PATTERNS**
(Paducah, KY: American Quilter's Society, 1989)
Over 4,000 block patterns identified and
categorized according to their geometric and
design properties.

**Harer, M.**
**THE ESSENTIAL GUIDE TO PRACTICALLY
PERFECT PATCHWORK: EVERYTHING YOU
NEED TO KNOW TO MAKE YOUR FIRST QUILT**
(Iola, WI: Krause Publications, 2002)
Starts with the basics of quilting and expands to
more advanced concepts.

**Holstein, J.**
**THE PIECED QUILT: AN AMERICAN DESIGN
TRADITION**
(New York: New York Graphic Society, 1973)
The definitive account of the history, traditions,
and significance of the American patchwork
quilt. The author is credited with the 1970s revival
of interest in the quilt and quiltmaking, as both
art and craft, which led to the current boom.

**Itten, J.**
**THE ART OF COLOR: THE SUBJECTIVE
EXPERIENCE AND OBJECTIVE RATIONALE OF
COLOR**
(New York: Van Nostrand Reinhold Co., 1969)
Exploration of the principles of color theory and
their applications.

**James, M.**
**THE QUILTMAKER'S HANDBOOK: A GUIDE TO
DESIGN AND CONSTRUCTION**
(Englewood Cliffs, NJ: Prentice-Hall, 1978)
After more than twenty years, this is still one of
the best and most comprehensive guides to
design, technique, and color, with very thorough
and detailed "how-to" instructions. Includes
guides to designing and drafting your own
blocks and making and using templates.

**James, M.**
**THE SECOND QUILTMAKER'S HANDBOOK:
CREATIVE APPROACHES TO CONTEMPORARY
QUILT DESIGN**
(Englewood Cliffs, NJ: Prentice-Hall, 1981)
Advanced advice and instruction on design and
practical quiltmaking; a sequel to the author's
first book.

**Khin, Y.**
**THE COLLECTOR'S DICTIONARY OF QUILT
NAMES AND PATTERNS**
(Washington, DC: Acropolis Books Ltd., 1980)
2,400 quilt blocks illustrated and described by
category and name.

**Malone, M.**
**1001 PATCHWORK DESIGNS**
(New York: Sterling Publishing Co. Inc., 1982)
Every block shown with construction lines and
shading. Indispensable.

**Speckmann, D.**
**PATTERN PLAY: CREATING YOUR
OWN QUILTS**
(Concord, CA: C&T Publishing, Inc., 1993)
An innovative approach to quilt design and
technique. Includes ways of adapting traditional
blocks or creating your own and using them in
quilts. Detailed and easy-to-follow instructions
and tips.

**Stockton, J.**
**DESIGNER'S GUIDE TO COLOR**
(San Francisco: Chronicle Books, 1984
[3 vols])
An indispensable practical guide to using color
and color combinations.

# Stockists and Manufacturers

## Thread

**COATS & CLARK**
30 Oatewood Drive, Suite 351
Greenville, SC 29615
864-234-0331
www.coatsandclark.com

**GÜTERMANN OF AMERICA**
P.O. Box 7387
Charlotte, NC 28241
888-488-3762
www.gutermann-us.com

**KREINIK MFG CO., INC.**
3106 Timanus Lane, Suite 101
Baltimore, MD 21244
800-537-2166
www.kreinik.com

**SULKY OF AMERICA**
3113 Broadpoint Drive
Harbor Heights, FL 33988
800-874-4115
www.sulky.com

**YLI CORPORATION**
161 West Main Street
Rock Hill, SC 29730
800-296-8139
www.ylicorp.com

## Sewing machine manufacturers

**BABY LOCK, USA**
1760 Gilsinn
St. Louis, MO 63026
800-422-2952
www.babylock.com

**BERNINA OF AMERICA, INC.**
3500 Thayer Court
Aurora, IL 60504
630-978-2500
www.berninausa.com

**BROTHER INTERNATIONAL**
100 Somerset Corporate
Boulevard
Bridgewater, NJ 08807
800-422-7684
www.brother.com

**ELNA USA**
1760 Gilsinn Lane
Fenton, MO 63026-0730
800-848-3562
www.elnausa.com

**HUSQVARNA VIKING SEWING MACHINES**
31000 Viking Parkway
Westlake, OH 44145
440-808-6550
www.husqvarnaviking.com

**JANOME AMERICA, INC.**
10 Industrial Avenue
Mahwah, NJ 07430
800-631-0183
www.janome.com

**PFAFF OF AMERICA**
31000 Viking Parkway
Westlake, OH 44145
800-997-3233
www.pfaff.com

## Quilting supplies

**CLOVER NEEDLECRAFT, INC.**
1007 East Dominguez Street #L
Carson, CA 90746
310-516-7846

**COLONIAL NEEDLE CO.**
74 Westmoreland Avenue
White Plains, NY 10606
914-946-7474
www.colonialneedle.com

**EZ QUILTING BY WRIGHTS**
85 South Street
West Warren, MA 01092
800-628-9362
www.ezquilt.com

**FISKARS, INC.**
7811 West Stewart Avenue
Wausau, WI 54401
www.fiskars.com

**OLFA PRODUCTS GROUP**
1536 Beech Street
Terre Haute, IN 47804
800-457-2665
www.olfa.com

**PRYM CONSUMER USA INC.**
P.O. Box 5028
Spartanburg, SC 29304
www.dritz.com

**THE WARM COMPANY**
854 East Union Street
Seattle, WA 98122
www.warmcompany.com

## Fabric manufacturers

**CRANSTON VILLAGE**
469 Seventh Avenue
New York, NY 10018
212-946-2202
www.cranstonvillage.com

**DAVID TEXTILES**
5959 Telegraph Road
City of Commerce, CA 90040
213-728-8231

**E.E. SCHENCK COMPANY**
P.O. Box 5200
Portland, OR 97208
800-433-0722
www.eeschenck.com

**MARCUS BROTHERS**
980 Avenue of the Americas
New York, NY 10018
212-354-8700
www.marcusbrothers.com

**P&B TEXTILES**
1580 Gilbreth Road
Burlingame, CA 94010
800-227-6338
www.pbtex.com

**ROBERT KAUFMAN FABRICS**
129 West 132nd Street
Los Angeles, CA 90061
800-877-2066

**SPRINGS INDUSTRIES**
420 East White Street
Rock Hill, SC 29730
www.springs.com

## Mail-order shopping

**CLOTILDE, INC.**
P.O. Box 7500
Big Sandy, TX 75755-7500
800-772-2891
Call for a free catalog
www.clotilde.com

**CONNECTING THREADS**
P.O. Box 8940
Vancouver, WA 98668-8940
800-574-6454
Call for a free catalog
www.connectingthreads.com

**HANCOCK'S OF PADUCAH**
3841 Hinkleville Road
Paducah, KY 42001
800-845-8723
Call for a free catalog
www.hancocks-paducah.com

# Index

# *Acknowledgments*

I would like to thank the following people:
My mother for all her help and encouragement, especially whilst I have been working on the book. My students past and present for their continued support, encouragement, and enthusiasm.

Quarto would like to thank and acknowledge the following for supplying quilts featured in the galleries.

**JANET COOK**
www.janetcook.co.uk
pages 25, 103, and 104. Collaborator with the author on Coral Reef, page 26.

**FRIEDA OXENHAM**
www.picturetrail.com/friedaquilter
page 59

All other quilts by the author.

Thank you also to the following shops and suppliers who kindly lent or gave materials and equipment.

**BERNINA SEWING MACHINES**
Bogod & Company Ltd.
50–52 Great Sutton Street
London EC1V 0DJ, United Kingdom
Tel: 0207 549 7849
www.bernina.co.uk

**THE BUTTON LADY**
Tel: 0121 329 3234
www.thebuttonlady.co.uk
By prior appointment only

**CREATIVE GRIDS (UK) LTD**
Leicester, United Kingdom
Tel: 0845 450 77 22/0845 450 77 33
Email: sales@creativegrids.com
www.creativegrids.com

**HANTEX LTD.**
Tel: 01754 820 800
Email: sales@hantex.co.uk

**MAKOWER FABRICS**
www.makoweruk.com

**OLIVER TWISTS**
22 Phoenix Road
Crowther, Washington, Tyne and Wear, NE38 0AD,
United Kingdom
Tel: 0191 4166016
Mail-order hand-dyed embroidery threads

**OUT OF AFRICA**
17 Bashford Way
Crawley, Sussex, RH10 7YF, United Kingdom
Mail order and shows, fabrics and threads

**SEW SIMPLE**
Unit 17, Taverham Garden Centre, Fir Covert Road
Norwich, Norfolk, NR8 6HT, United Kingdom
Tel: 01603 262 870
www.sewsimpleonline.co.uk